You
Understanding Sleep, Dr
Hypnosis

By Victor Garlock, Ph.D.

Copyright © 2012 by Victor Garlock

Published and distributed by
Possibilities Publishing Co.
PO Box 10671
Burke, VA 22009

www.possibilitiespublishingcompany.com

Contents

Contents 2

Preamble 4

Introduction...8

Chapter 1
Hypnosis Solves a Crime...12

Chapter 2
Hypnosis Briefly Defined 22

Chapter 3
Hypnosis Through the Ages 25

Chapter 4
Early Self-Hypnosis...40

Chapter 5
The Power of the Unconscious Mind 42

Chapter 6
Self-Hypnosis 55

Chapter 7
Storytelling 69

Chapter 8
Sleep 76

Chapter 9
A Night's Journey 87

Chapter 10
Day/Night People..98

Chapter 11
The Sleepwalker Killing 104

Chapter 12
Sleep Disorders...112

Chapter 13
Dreams and the Unconscious Mind...125

Chapter 14
Dreams, Ancient Understandings 130

Chapter 15
Freud and Jung..134

Chapter 16
Dream Work 140

Chapter 17
ESP 168

Chapter 18
The Transformation of a Dream 178

Chapter 19
Dreams Through the Stages of Life...187

Chapter 20
The Dreams of Prisoners and Mathematicians 191

Chapter 21
Brain Chemistry and Spiritual Awakening....................................198

Preamble

"I was sitting in a lawn chair by the pool on our back deck. I was certain that there was no way that our 2-year-old son, Jason, could open the door between the family room and the deck. My husband had devised a latch that was out of Jason's reach. So I could rest easily reading a book while enjoying the sunshine.

"I heard the back door open and looked to see if my husband John was about to join me. I was shocked to see Jason toddling across the deck headed straight for the pool, where a floating beach ball had attracted his attention. 'How in the world did he get out?' I asked myself.

"I attempted to get up, only to find that I was unable to move. I began to panic as Jason toddled closer to the pool. Still, I was unable to move. I decided to holler for John. But no sound came out of my mouth. My panic grew into complete and total terror as I found myself sitting bolt upright in my bed with cold sweat on my face and chest.

"It was about 4 a.m. and the house was quiet as I tried to settle back down. But sleep was impossible, so I decided to get up and get something to drink and walk around to calm my nerves. Then it occurred to me to check the door that in the dream Jason had opened by himself in order to get out onto the patio. Much to my surprise, when I pushed on the door it opened easily. A cold shiver ran down my spine as I realized that the locking mechanism had worked its way loose and was no longer functioning properly.

"John was a little put off that I was awakening him in the middle of the night, but when I showed him the door he was stunned into full wakefulness. He went and got some tools and performed the repairs on the spot and decided that he would add a second latch the next morning."

In this dream, Janice received a warning about impending disaster.

Janice was eager to share this dream in one of my sleep and dreams classes. She wondered aloud about where the information in this dream had come from, information that may have saved her son's life.

In another one of my sleep and dreams classes, a continuing education student in her 40s dreamed that a rat had bitten her just to the right of the nipple on her left breast. She and her husband owned a small farm, and there had recently been an infestation of rats in one of the barns where they kept grain for their horses. They had acquired a couple of cats to deal with the problem, and the day before the dream there had been a number of dead rats strewn around near the barn. Ruth thought that the dream was just a nightmare related to those unpleasant images.

She was in the habit of periodically doing a self-breast examination, and it occurred to her to check out that particular area especially carefully. She found an almost undetectable lump in the very spot where the dream rat had bitten her. This discovery led to an unusually early detection of a malignant breast tumor.

Norman was not the typical student who was likely to enroll in my Wednesday evening sleep and dreams class. During the round of introductions that is part of the first class, Norman shared that he was a long-distance truck driver and might have to miss a class or two when he was on the road.

Norman was obviously comfortable enough with himself that he was not embarrassed about taking a sleep and dreams course that he himself described as "kind of funny around the edges." But I wondered what had motivated him to sign up.

Before long we had our answer. Norman was an identical twin, and after a few classes he began to describe how he and his twin brother had over the years experienced many incidents of what he called "being in each other's head."

His mother had told the twins many stories, he said, about how, when they were separated as infants or toddlers, one of them would react if the other had fallen down or in other ways was in distress. Norman reported that during childhood they had many incidents of seeming to share the same dream. He said they often talked about dreams at the breakfast table, assuming that the other one would fill in the details.

According to Norman, a recent and dramatic example was when his twin brother Tom, who was a runner, dreamed that he had had to drop out of a 10K race with severe leg cramps. He woke up with violent leg spasms. He described them as excruciating. He had never had even minor cramps before.

That same morning the brakes had failed on the rig that Norman was driving and he had to use an emergency runaway truck pull-off. The landing didn't go well and both of Norman's legs were broken. Neither Norman nor Tom could be persuaded that these two concurring incidents were a coincidence.

All of these dreamers had been so impressed by the apparent intelligence of their inner mind that they wanted to learn more. That was why they had enrolled in my sleep and dreams class.

This book is, in a sense, a response to their questions and the questions of the many people out there who have had similar experiences that have made them wonder about the wonders of the inner mind.

Author's Notes:

First, readers should know that none of the cases described in this book are actual specific patients, students or group members. Instead, these cases are a composite of the experiences of a number of different people. This has been done to protect the anonymity of the people I have worked with and also to add color and interest to the text with stories that grab the reader's attention while remaining true to my cumulative observations and work over the years.

Second, I want readers to know that I have established an active website: www.hypnosisdreams.com. It provides additional information and forums for discussions about topics in the areas of sleep, dreams, hypnosis and self-hypnosis as well as self-hypnosis recordings I have prepared for you to use for your self-help projects. These self-hypnosis recorded scripts include topics such as: improving dream recall, quitting smoking, getting better sleep, and sticking to a healthy diet, among many others.

Introduction

As we will learn later, the first two examples in the preamble can be explained through an understanding of the way that the unconscious mind can sometimes be more observant than the conscious mind. While we are going about our business during the day, our conscious mind may be too busy to notice details in the environment. But the unconscious mind may not only register the information but then incorporate it into a dream that night. Such an explanation does not have to resort to claims of special mental telepathy abilities.

By including the third report of Norman's incident of extrasensory communication between him and his twin brother, I don't intend to say that this kind of episode is all that common. Nor do I want to emphasize the mental telepathy aspects of human consciousness. There is so much about the depths of our minds that is fascinating, even if we are tempted to disbelieve extraordinary claims such as those made by Norman and others.

That being said, we will in a later chapter discuss the claims of extrasensory perception that come up frequently among those who regularly remember their dreams. In fact, many people who had been skeptics about such things become much less sure of their skepticism once they begin to remember and share their dreams with others. In fact, in that later chapter we will examine some pretty convincing evidence about extrasensory perception. But those kinds of issues are only a small part of what this book is about.

This book is about the remarkable windows we can open into our unconscious minds. It is about freeing some of our deep life-giving energy so that it can enrich and enliven our experience of being alive. In the process, we will expand our understanding of ourselves and the people around us.

As you continue reading, you will enter an adventure into the worlds of hypnosis, sleep and dreams. These three aspects of being alive show us how much of our mental power we are usually unaware of during our everyday lives.

Much more is now known about these three alternate states of consciousness than even a few decades ago. So prepare to be stimulated and enlightened. In addition, you'll learn self-hypnosis, guided imagery and dream work techniques that will enable you to gain more access into the richness and wisdom of your inner mind.

The first seven chapters of this book deal with hypnosis and self-hypnosis. Many people would say that hypnosis is a baffling, magical, even miraculous state of mind. And they would be right. Even after we separate myth from reality, hypnosis remains impressive. It provides us a window into the unconscious mind. It is also impressive because it gives us a tool for tapping into those powers and freeing them to flow forth. In these chapters, we will recount the fascinating history of hypnosis over the centuries. You'll read dramatic examples of the effects possible with hypnosis. You will also be taught a number of self-hypnotic techniques to deepen your connection with your unconscious mind and help you improve your life.

In chapters 8 through 13, we will talk about sleep. Every night, we all enter the mysterious world of sleep. We tend to take each night's journey for granted because it is so familiar. It is, of course, during these hours of sleep that dreams are woven into existence. But there is much more to this alternate universe than the islands of dreaming that appear there. Gaining knowledge of this other world, where we spend almost a third of our lives, will bring us understanding and increased self awareness.

We will explore the predictable pattern of a night's sleep. You'll learn about sleep cycles and the different stages of sleep, including the stage where dreams are created. Other topics will include a startling example of violent sleepwalking; cases of sleepers who act out their dreams; people who suffer from a disorder that throws them into unconsciousness right in the middle of the day; and an extreme form of insomnia that runs in families and always results in death.

Chapters 14 through 20 will be our adventure into the land of dreams. Dreams are a rich treasure, a gift from what seems like another world. They come from the same places in us as the ideas of geniuses, the same places from where the world's great creative masterpieces have sprung. Learning how to remember and understand dreams will enrich your life.

You will discover how dreams have been understood through the ages. You will learn about more recent psychological ideas about dreams. And then we will discuss the best ways to work with dreams to release their liberating influence into our waking lives. You will learn techniques for really sinking your teeth into, appreciating and understanding your dreams. Even if you never practice these techniques, reading these chapters will give you more contact with your reservoir of inner wisdom, making it more available to you.

Some of the content of your dreams arises out of your unique individual unconscious mind. In addition, however, dreams come from a place deep inside of us that we share with all of humanity. This place has been called the collective unconscious. Each night in our dreams we revisit our ancient common ancestors. Their dreams have become our dreams. Our dream landscapes are from their world. And many of our dream characters share a common origin rooted in our ancestral history. Because of these ancient collective memories, we have more in common with each other than we think. So being in touch with dreams reminds us of our common bonds and nourishes our collective life.

Some dreams contain a lot of this collective content. Carl Jung, the famous psychologist, called such dreams "big dreams." Such dreams are usually very vivid and emotionally gripping and may haunt you all day or even longer. Working with these dreams can be especially productive. People with a strong spiritual life often describe these dreams as inspirational and helpful in their prayer life.

You will learn how our dreams change over the course of a lifetime. The dreams of the elderly are quite different than those during childhood. Understanding where you are in your life and how your dreams relate to that reality can be very enlightening.

You'll learn about the dreams of criminals at a maximum security prison. Some dramatic examples may surprise you. An interesting case of the dreams of a brilliant mathematician will demonstrate how our life passions show up in our dreams.

Before we go further, it is important to tell you what this book is not about. This book is not about you doing psychotherapy upon yourself. It is about gaining knowledge and understanding, the enrichment of your psychological life and the pleasure of self-exploration.

Neither is this book about trying to gain control over your unconscious mind. Your inner mind has an intelligence and a creativity of its own, and to try to bully it would be to insult the deepest parts of your being. Instead, our goal is to help you to free more of the creative energies within you to flow more naturally into your everyday life.

There are times, however, when the unconscious mind can get stuck in a kind of destructive feedback loop and needs soothing guidance from the conscious mind. People suffering from post-traumatic stress disorder experience this reality. Traumatic incidents from decades ago can still be exerting a powerful negative influence on the victim's current life.

In a chapter on self-hypnosis, you will learn techniques that have proven very useful for anyone whose inner mind seems to be caught in re-living traumatic experiences from the past.

These techniques are also helpful for people stuck in chronic worry or regret or for people who can't stop themselves from compulsively focusing on anxious or depressing thoughts.

So let us begin our explorations into the richness of the unconscious mind and the three roads of hypnosis, sleep and dreams that lead into its depths. We'll begin traveling the first road by uncovering the secrets of hypnosis and self-hypnosis.

Chapter 1

Hypnosis Solves a Crime

In the early 1970s, a law enforcement agency located in a community near where I had just begun a part-time hypnosis practice got wind of my interest in using hypnosis in criminal investigation. Investigators were working on what was becoming a cold case. About eight months earlier, Lisa, a college coed, had been raped in an especially brutal way by a man who had picked her up while she was hitchhiking. The rapist had taken her into a wooded area and repeatedly assaulted her for almost 18 hours. In between the assaults, he had kept her bound and gagged in the trunk of his car.

In spite of the fact that the victim had spent so much time in the custody of the rapist, and in spite of the fact that he hadn't worn a mask of any kind, she could not provide even a sketchy description of him. Neither was she able to provide a useful description of the vehicle that he drove. She couldn't say for sure whether it was a two-door or four-door or what color it was. The investigating officers said that she was so calm and matter-of-fact when talking about the crime that if it had not been for her severe injuries, there would have been considerable doubt about whether or not a crime had actually been committed.

I ended up working with Lisa and the results were so dramatic that they had a profound effect upon the investigation. The experience also changed my own ideas about the power of hypnosis itself. What I confirmed then and since is that hypnosis is a way of opening a door into your inner mind

Hypnosis and the Law

Before I proceed to describe the hypnosis session with Lisa, I want to give you some background information about where I was in my developing career as a hypnotist and also the legal status of hypnosis in criminal cases.

In about 1971, I first learned the basics of becoming a practicing hypnotist from a course designed by Harry Arons, a pioneer in the modern-day use of hypnosis. Later, I happened to run into Harry one evening following a long day of sessions at an annual hypnosis convention. Harry and I were unwinding in the hotel lounge and struck up a conversation. He was a strong advocate for the ethical use of hypnosis and, at the time, he was especially active in promoting the use of hypnosis in law enforcement and criminal investigation. We visited for over an hour and talked mostly about that emerging interest of his. He was always a storehouse of information and insight, and his creative and innovative way of approaching hypnosis was contagious.

I was just developing my private hypnosis practice and my chance encounter with Harry really got my juices going. I wanted to get a chance to work in the area of law enforcement. I followed up by reading some material Harry had sent me. At the time, he was working on expanding this material into a textbook.

I had learned that the ability of some people under hypnosis to remember details of events thought to be forgotten can be useful in law enforcement. There have been dramatic cases of witnesses remembering details like license plate numbers. These details have sometimes led to the apprehension of criminals. Interestingly, the courts do not allow the testimony of witnesses who have been hypnotized because such witnesses can become so convinced of the correctness of their memories that they are difficult to cross-examine. The courts have ruled that this gives the prosecution an undue advantage.

In the case of Lisa's rape, the investigators requested that I try to use hypnosis to get her to recall useful details because the investigation had totally stalled. Although I really wanted to do this kind of work, I was reluctant for a number of reasons.

First of all, I was a novice hypnotist and wasn't really sure that I had the confidence to bring true expertise to the challenge at hand. Second was my concern that criminal courts were already making decisions calling into question the reliability of witnesses and victims of crimes who had been hypnotized. As mentioned above, courts questioned whether hypnotized subjects would maintain a kind of certainty about their memory that was unjustified and even downright wrong. In addition, there was concern that the hypnotist might make subtle suggestions leading the hypnotic subject in the wrong direction. So I warned the investigators that any information we gleaned would not be usable in court.

My third misgiving was the most serious. Lisa was clearly engaging in what is called repression. So overwhelming was the experience of the crime that deep within her mind she had made a very wise decision to totally forget the entire terrifying series of events. All surrounding information had also been flushed down the repression drain.

In regard to my initial reluctance about my lack of experience, the investigating officers responded correctly that I probably was the only show in town. Either they would ask me to give it a shot or forget the whole thing. And they really felt that this might be the only way to move the case forward. In regard to my second objection, about hypnosis testimony being inadmissible in court, they decided that, since the investigation was completely stalled, the risk was worth taking.

They wanted to keep the whole enterprise under wraps. I agreed to complete secrecy and to not even share the enterprise with colleagues who might be helpful. Investigators were concerned that the press might get wind of what we were doing and create an atmosphere that would indeed interfere with possible future legal proceedings. Hypnosis has recently become much more legitimate in its reputation, but in the 1960s and 70s it still had an air of the occult.

In regard to my third concern, about the emotional dangers of removing Lisa's repression, Harry Arons and I had discussed a technique wherein the hypnotized victim is regressed to the time of the crime but in a manner that is at least twice removed. I did some research and came up with a plan. But I really was uncomfortable proceeding unless the young woman saw a psychiatrist at least once before we began. I wanted to get a clinical opinion about the safety of proceeding. She agreed to that stipulation. The psychiatrist that I suggested was someone who had already referred a few of his patients to me for specific hypnotic treatment, so I knew that he was someone who understood the usefulness and authenticity of hypnosis. He gave us the go-ahead. Of course, anything Lisa said to the psychiatrist was kept confidential, in keeping with doctor-patient confidentiality. So the law enforcement officers were reassured regarding secrecy.

With Lisa's consent, the entire session would be recorded with both video and audio. With the equipment set up, and with most of the law enforcement agency's staff arrayed around the room, Lisa settled in on a sofa with pillows arranged to help her get comfortable.

Lisa's Hypnosis

So this is what the session looked like. First I asked her to tell me about herself in general, and we spent a lot of time discussing family, friends, college, and so on. She was taking a lot of biology, anatomy and physiology courses in preparation for trying to get into a graduate program in veterinary medicine. She knew why I was working with her and understood that we were going to proceed with hypnosis, but she was in no hurry to get started. She was more than content to just shoot the breeze. And I was in no hurry either.

Eventually we began to talk about her memories from the day of the attack. She said that she had attended a morning class and then had walked from the college to a friend's house nearby. After that, she started hitchhiking to her sister's house a few miles out of town. That was the last thing she remembered clearly. She described every memory after that as pretty much a blur.

One of the things that I had already learned from my hypnosis practice was that some especially receptive hypnotic subjects can begin to go into hypnosis during regular conversation. This is what began to happen with Lisa. So as she began to get drowsy I suggested that she close her eyes and begin to drift into a quiet, relaxed hypnotic place.

Then I began to talk slowly and calmly to deepen her hypnotic state. I was a little nervous, so I tried to sound as relaxed and calm as possible. I could see that Lisa's breathing had slowed, and I could see the subtle reflections of her heart rate in her face and neck, indicating that her pulse rate was also slowing.

It was now time to construct the layers of protection to prevent Lisa from being overwhelmed by any memories that we might be able to help her dig up. So I told her that she was about to enter a private movie theater in her imagination. This movie theater was just for her and was a safe and private place. In this movie theater, she was the one who could start or stop what was taking place on the screen.

I began slowly leading her through a series of memories that had nothing to do with the crime. After almost an hour, she was still enjoying relaxing scenes of herself with her family and friends at home and at a summer cottage on a nearby lake she had told me about. I prolonged one scene, where she was playing with her dog, for about 15 minutes. She had earlier talked about how much she enjoyed playing tug-of-war and fetch with him.

Finally, I was able to push through my own reluctance and began the actual work at hand. I told her that she was going to watch a movie of a man and a woman hitchhiker he had just picked up. I told her that these were not people that she in any way knew. The man was a stranger and so was the woman. In addition I told her that these were not real people but were actors playing their parts.

I then began to take her through the day, piecing together information from what I already knew. I asked her to give me a certain hand signal if she experienced any anxiety at all and another signal if the anxiety became painful.

So we began. I had earlier established that she could respond to questions that I would ask her. Responding to questions would not bring her out of hypnosis, but the sound of her own voice would actually take her more deeply into trance. After I set the stage, I asked her to become the screenwriter and to move the script forward as she thought it should go to be realistic and good and thrilling entertainment. Then I remained quiet while she described the action on the screen.

She began with a general description of what was going on between the couple. Then she said that the girl was getting nervous because the driver was taking her in a different direction than she wanted to go. He had reassured her that he just had an errand to run and then would drive her back to where she was headed. Then she described how the girl asked to be let out of the car, saying she would find a different ride. At this point, she said, the man pulled out a knife.

Even though she hadn't given me the anxiety signal, I stopped Lisa and asked her if the movie was upsetting her at all. She said no, that she was finding it interesting and was excited about what might happen next. She added that as a child she had always liked scary movies. She said her sisters would run out of the TV room and hold their hands over their ears. But she would just laugh and really enjoyed the thrill of it all. This was something that turned out to be a major asset in our work.

She then described how the assailant had pulled off into an isolated wooded area and stopped the car. I told her that if at any time she wanted to slow down or stop the action she could do so. She said she was already doing that in order to see the details of what was happening. I asked her if she could see the man's face clearly on the screen. She said that she couldn't. But then she said that she could read the girl's mind and the girl had a perfect view of the man's face. Lisa said that the girl had always imagined that she might be the victim of a crime. She had told herself that if that ever happened she would make every effort to remember as many details as possible in order to help the police apprehend the criminal.

Lisa then began to talk about the next scene without following through on the girl's description of her assailant. So I stopped her and asked if she could share with me what she was receiving from the girl's mind. She laughed and said that she forgot that I was there for a minute. But now that I had reminded her, she would tell me what the girl was sharing with her. She then gave me a detailed description of the man.

At one point, it was clear that she had jumped forward in time to when she was actually being assaulted. I could tell because she described the man's face as right on top of her's so that she was looking directly into his eyes. She described the color of his eyes with speckles of a slightly different color. She described his skin coloring, the color of his hair, the pattern of his beard, the size of his nose, the fact that he had a couple of crooked top teeth and one missing bottom tooth.

I was blown away by the detail of her description. The law enforcement officers were barely able to contain themselves while listening to all these details.

A little later, I asked Lisa if the girl was conveying to her any information about the car. Her descriptions of the car were as detailed as her description of the assailant. She remembered the interior with impeccable detail, including a couple of cracks in the upholstery on the passenger side, a number of coffee or other stains on the floor carpeting, and a small crack in the windshield just to the side of the rear view mirror. She remembered the exterior with a little less detail, but she described the color as a weathered light blue. She apparently knew enough about paint to recognize that it had been poorly repainted and that a spot had been missed between the trunk and the right tail light.

The detail of her memory was truly impressive and couldn't have been farther removed from the total amnesia that she had displayed before hypnosis. Our entire session took over three hours. I was pretty tired but Lisa was very willing to continue longer. She was definitely enjoying the adventure, as hard as that was for me to believe considering how traumatized she had been.

I had decided before our session that no matter what information we got, running the risk of Lisa remembering any of it afterwards was not going to be wise. So I told her that we were going to bring the movie to a close. I told her we were going to return to movies of her life with her friends and family. She was disappointed at first and wanted to continue what she called her "thriller movie." She said she felt like she had as a teenager, enjoying the rush of being a little scared but much less scared than the people around her.

With some apparent regret, she went along with my killjoy attitude and watched some calm lighthearted footage for a while. I then had an idea that I thought might help the transition into establishing her amnesia, which I was sure was absolutely necessary to protect her. So I reminded her that sometimes people fall asleep during a movie, especially if it is kind of boring, which she had already said her family movies were becoming. So while she was watching those movies, I monotonously suggested that she would get groggy and begin to lose consciousness and drift off to sleep where she would begin to dream. In her dream, she would remember that she had had an earlier dream of going to the movies. But now that earlier dream was fading and would soon be forgotten as dreams often are.

I repeated many times that she would have no recall of any of the movies she had watched. I was in no hurry to end the session at this point because I was concerned that my suggestions for renewed repression might not have completely taken hold. I feared she might wake up and be overwhelmed by those memories. It turned out that I needn't have worried because she woke up from hypnosis with no recall of the "movie" that she had produced and directed.

With my encouragement, Lisa decided to enter psychotherapy and over a period of about a year and a half she was able to gradually recall her ordeal. It was important to her to remember what had happened. She was a courageous young woman and with professional help and family support she was able to lift the veil of repression and integrate her memories into her conscious mind.

The Investigation

Following our session, I was still concerned about the mental state of our young subject. But she seemed to be fine. We had agreed beforehand that she would not be viewing the video that we had made. I had also insisted that she not be further questioned by any of the detectives for at least a week and, even then, none of the material gained during the session was to be brought up.

The investigators were guardedly excited about the whole thing. And we all wondered if what we heard were actual memories or the fabrication of a vivid imagination. It didn't take long to find out because an artist's sketch of the face that Lisa had so meticulously described produced a hit almost right away. An investigator in a nearby jurisdiction had recently arrested the suspect in a case of domestic assault. A visit to the suspect's home turned up a car exactly matching the description in Lisa's movie.

The perpetrator was never brought to trial for his crime against Lisa. But he was convicted of a similar crime that had been committed earlier. Investigators had already accumulated some evidence in the other case and the new information further pinned things down. They were able to put together a lineup for the earlier victim, who picked out her attacker with no doubt. It was the same assailant. So, based on the information Lisa had provided, this man was brought to justice even though it was for a different crime. He died in prison some years later.

I have always been grateful for the lucky coming together of my meeting with Harry Arons and the request for help from law enforcement. I was a young and not fully convinced practitioner of hypnosis. I had learned the art of hypnotizing, but I was not yet a true believer in the depths to which hypnosis can go in tapping into the unconscious mind. This case settled the issue for me once and for all. And the confidence it gave me has strengthened my ability to use hypnosis to help people in many different ways for almost four decades.

This case is a dramatic example of how effective hypnosis can be in restoring memory. I have worked with many people to improve memory for academic and a variety of personal reasons. There have also been a few especially interesting cases, such as a woman who had buried some jewelry and cash in her backyard during a nasty divorce. She had written down directions to find the items later only to have misplaced them. After the divorce was complete, she came to me for help in the hopes of retrieving her treasures. Using hypnosis and self-hypnosis, she was successful.

Later, when we discuss techniques of self-hypnosis, I will share with you some effective techniques for improving memory for whatever other purposes would be of value in your life.

Having now read an example of the power of hypnosis, you might be interested in finding out exactly what hypnosis is. Even hypnotists who have used hypnotic techniques for years have a hard time explaining it. So, in the next chapter, we'll take a shot at trying to pin down this elusive state of consciousness.

Chapter 2

Hypnosis Briefly Defined

So what is hypnosis anyway?

Hypnosis is a natural state that all of us go in and out of every day. Whenever you zone out on something, you're in a kind of hypnosis. Listening to music, getting lost in conversation and spacing out while driving a car are all hypnotic experiences.

Let's look at a naturally occurring episode of hypnosis that you've probably experienced many times. You walk into a movie theater and sit down with your popcorn. You know that you are about to see a spectacle that's entirely pretend. You know that the people you will see on the screen are actors and actresses who are following a script. You also know that the scenery and the special effects are not real. Beyond that, you also know that you're sitting in a room of illusion. The actors you're seeing are not really there but are produced through the technology of modern cinema.

But in spite of all of that knowledge, you make a decision to accept it all as real and, as you begin watching, you let yourself be captured into the grip of it. You are in hypnosis. And because you're in hypnosis, these artificial happenings can make you laugh, jump with surprise, cry or get angry. And all of these emotional states can be measured by attaching equipment that measures your biological reactions. And those reactions prove to be as real as they would be if the events you are watching on the screen were actually happening in reality. That is hypnosis. It's not mysterious. It's not magic. It's not supernatural. It occurs all the time.

Having said all that, it's also true that there is much more to the story. What about a person like Lisa, who remembered every detail of an event that previously had seemed to be totally forgotten? What about volunteers in a stage hypnosis demonstration who swat at imaginary mosquitoes or stand and salute an imaginary flag, or laugh and blush because they think everybody in the audience is naked? Or what about eastern yogis who, through practicing focus and concentration, can endure extreme temperatures or painful events without seeming to experience any discomfort?

And what about the over 3,000 Chinese young men who in 1984, despite all evidence to the contrary, thought that their penis was shrinking and that they were in danger of dying as a result? (These men were caught up in an epidemic of Koro, a psychological condition specific to Chinese culture) And what about the 34 people in Fort Worth, Texas, who in 2009 were taken to the hospital with all the symptoms of carbon monoxide poisoning? Afterward, it was discovered that they were not exposed to carbon monoxide at all and that their symptoms were completely self-created. And what about the miracle cures of faith healing and exorcisms?

So how can we explain both the everyday experience of getting lost in a movie or television show and the more dramatic examples just mentioned?

Psychologists still have arguments about what exactly hypnosis is. Since you are going to be using self-hypnosis, let's take a look at the different ways that hypnosis is currently thought of.

One long-held point of view is that hypnosis is an altered state of consciousness. Just as sleep is an altered state of consciousness, or being under the influence of alcohol, so hypnosis is its own special state. According to this view, the key to using hypnosis or self-hypnosis is to find a way to get into this state and stay there long enough to have positive benefits. Focused concentration is thought to be important in inducing the state. Gazing at a candle or staring at a moving watch or metronome might do the trick.

A second point of view understands hypnosis as a kind of role-playing. This is not to say that the hypnotized subject is faking, but rather that he is getting so deeply into the role of being hypnotized that dramatic things happen.

For stage actors, a distinction is sometimes drawn between technical acting and what's called heated acting. In technical acting, the actor is always aware that he is acting and consciously engages in his craft. The heated actor, in contrast, tries to lose himself in the role and become the person whom he is playing. Hypnosis might be seen as a form of heated acting. The role becomes so real that dramatic changes in behavior can result.

There is an expression in Alcoholics Anonymous that says, "Fake it until you make it." Following that advice would be a good idea according to the role-playing theory of hypnosis. Go ahead and pretend that you feel no pain in your injured foot. As long as you're getting appropriate medical care, you just might, with proper hypnotic techniques, be able to convince yourself that you do indeed feel no pain, and the pain will vanish like a forgotten memory.

A third point of view is that hypnosis is about belief and expectation. It's a little like some of the experiments that have shown that if marijuana smokers believe that a cigarette contains active THC, some of them will get stoned even if no active intoxicant is in the weed. This is also related to what's called the placebo effect in which, for example, some patients experience pain relief from a sugar pill they think is morphine.

How exactly to understand hypnosis will probably always be open to debate. The history of hypnosis, to which we turn our attention in the next chapter, demonstrates that it has long been a powerful yet often baffling state of consciousness.

Chapter 3

Hypnosis Through the Ages

The term hypnosis was unknown in the ancient world. However, there were many things going on that we would now explain by using the language of hypnosis.

Physicians in ancient Egypt sometimes used magic mirrors to induce what they considered a special kind of sleep in their patients. Healing that took place under the influence of these mirrors was thought to be more effective. In ancient Greece and Egypt, as well as in Persia, suffering people would go to sleep temples to be put into a sleep state in order to be healed. A contemporary of Aristotle's described a young boy whose painful symptoms were relieved by passing a special stick over his body. It was said that for a while his soul left his body and during that time he was insensitive to pain. That sounds like hypnosis to me. Unfortunately, the pain returned when his soul re-entered his body.

Many of the miraculous healings that took place during the first few hundred years of Christianity might be explained, at least in part, as individual or group hypnosis. And certainly, the mass hysteria that was stirred up around the issue of witchcraft during the Middle Ages was hypnotic in nature.

But probably the first well-known hypnotic practitioner was a priest who considered what he was doing to be spiritual. Looking back, it was almost surely a kind of hypnosis.

Exorcism or Hypnosis

In the 1700s, Johann Joseph Gassner was an Austrian parish priest and flamboyant exorcist. As a young priest, Father Gassner had been stricken with a series of ailments that were persistent and did not respond to the standard medical treatment of the time. Gassner developed the idea that his illness was not a medical condition at all but a spiritual one, the result of demon possession.

Father Gassner prayed long and hard and read up on the history of demon possession and earlier procedures of exorcism. He came up with his own special technique, which he applied to himself with miraculous success. As a result, he became convinced that he could use his technique to heal other lost sinners who were under the sway of the devil.

The good father was quite the showman. He was a kind of 18th-century televangelist and faith healer. He attracted large crowds, and his healings were dramatic and crowd-pleasing.

Just 100 years earlier, the Roman Catholic Church was full of exorcisms and witch hunters. But by the time Gassner came along, the church had come under the influence of the Enlightenment, and such activities were considered questionable at best. However, many members of the general population considered the Enlightenment to be an unwanted intellectual intrusion into their experience of the divine and the demonic. This Counter-Enlightenment movement had widespread popular support. Father Gassner became one of its spokespersons and rock stars.

Gassner's exorcisms were different from earlier exorcisms in a couple of key ways. First, he was not intervening on behalf of poor souls who were displaying classic signs of demon possession, such as speaking strange tongues, ranting and raving, cursing God and Jesus, and otherwise acting out the will of the demon through their behavior and their voices.

Gassner's victims of demon possession were simply suffering from one kind of illness or another. His argument was that such everyday illnesses were also the result of unwanted intrusions from Satan's demons.

Secondly, the exorcisms were done publicly and performed on multiple souls in the presence of large throngs of witnesses.

Gassner's reputation spread throughout Europe. He was attacked by many who had come to view the world through the philosophical lens of the Enlightenment and who believed that his theology and his methods were a throwback to a superstitious and dangerous era. There was evidence that at least one witch trial was inspired by Gassner's revival of demon possession as a believed reality.

Gassner would begin his ritualistic exorcism by questioning the gathered Christians regarding the state of their beliefs in salvation and the divinity of Jesus. Once he established that he was dealing with true believers, he would proceed with the exorcism through the laying on of hands and repetitive rhythmic prayers.

His parishioners would often seem to faint or develop seizures or scream out loud, or in other ways display the power of what was going on. Sometimes, Father Gassner would command the evil spirit to move from one part of the body to another and the person would cry out in agony as the demon had its way with his body. Gassner would then command in the name of Christ that the demon depart from the victim. He would often physically pull victims' arms, massaging the demon down toward the fingertips and then out into the ether where it could no longer torment.

Magnetism or Hypnosis

There was another flamboyant healer operating in Europe at the same time. Franz Anton Mesmer had a very different way of healing the afflicted. At least it seemed very different. We might now look back and say that both of these healers were using hypnosis but dressed in different clothing.

Mesmer was a physician and had developed a theory of how illness and health operated. Mesmer, who believed he was expanding human scientific knowledge, proposed that there was a subtle magnetic fluid in the human body. He had, early in his career, developed an interest in astrology and was influenced by astrologers who attempted to account for the way in which heavenly bodies were believed to determine human behavior and destiny.

It had long been known that the position of the moon is what, through its magnetic force, causes the ocean tides. There also had developed a belief that the moon phase had a profound effect upon human behavior. The full moon was blamed for many symptoms of mental illness. In fact, the word lunatic is derived from the word lunar, meaning moon. Mesmer believed that it was also through magnetic influence that the stars and planets have their effect.

Mesmer reasoned that if magnetic influence can have an effect from as far away as the moon and the planets, how much more powerful would it be when it's close-up and personal? His theory and the therapeutic techniques based on it came to be known as animal magnetism.

Mesmer's public demonstrations of the power of magnetism were similar in their mood, results and showmanship to the revival meetings, healings and exorcisms conducted by Johan Gassner. The difference, of course, was in the nature of the explanation for these dramatic healings. Gassner explained them as the influence of spiritual purity upon demonic forces. Mesmer explained them as the result of the correction of magnetic disturbances in the subtle fluids of the body by a healer who possessed a strong magnetic force. Mesmer also drew parallels between magnetic fluids and the metallic magnetic theories that were being developed at the time. Mesmer became so well-known that we still use the word mesmerized to describe someone who has been entranced.

Exorcism, Magnetism or Hypnosis

It was only a matter of time before these two world views clashed in the persons of these-two men. Mesmer came to believe that Father Gassner was, without realizing it, practicing magnetic therapy. Mesmer reasoned that the parish priest was so charismatic because he was a magnetically powerful person. His very presence could bring about changes in someone with weak magnetic powers. And then, according to Mesmer, when Gassner would practice the laying on of hands, the magnetic force became even more focused and effective in bringing about a cure. These healings were often accompanied by fainting and sometimes seizures. Since these reactions were often seen by Mesmer in his own patients, he saw them as further evidence that Gassner was unknowingly practicing animal magnetism.

Mesmer was invited by the Munich Academy of Sciences to give his opinion regarding the exorcisms of Father Gassner. His view that Gassner was really practicing animal magnetism carried the day and essentially discredited the priest. Still, there were masses of followers and believers who continued to flock to Gassner's healings and exorcisms undaunted by the alleged evidence of science.

Following a well-publicized failure to cure a young famous pianist of her blindness, Mesmer decided to move his practice from Austria to Paris, where there was much more notoriety and wealth to be had. He started a practice in a kind of healing salon. At first, Mesmer's healings were performed on one person at a time. The transfer of his own animal magnetism to a patient often took several hours of physical contact to accomplish. As Mesmer's reputation grew, masses of patients flocked to his salon. In order to treat groups of patients at one time, he constructed a device called a baquet, around which as many as 20 patients could be treated. He had four baquets located in four different rooms so that upwards of 200 people could be treated each day.

The baquet was an elaborately decorated covered circular wooden tub of water. Mesmer claimed that the device could store some of his animal magnetism. In addition to water, the baquet contained metal filings and ground glass to increase its magnetic properties. Patients were arranged around the baquet and linked together with a rope, each in contact with a metal rod protruding from the baquet. Mesmer would then sashay quietly into the room wearing flowing robes and slippers decorated with golden threads. His mere entrance into the room would re-magnetize the baquet and occasion many of his patients to experience dramatic seizures. The seizures were a sign of the crisis that was necessary in order to correct the magnetic imbalance and restore a healthy flow of magnetic fluid in the suffering patient.

There was such an outpouring of desire for Mesmer's magnetic treatment that, in order to placate the crowds that gathered outside, he agreed to magnetize a tree in the courtyard where the poor could gather and receive the benefits of Mesmer's miracle scientific cure. The fact that a tree is not something that can truly be magnetized seems to not have troubled Mesmer or his patients.

Mesmer gathered detractors, and even enemies, over the years until finally there was an investigation of his practices. There were those who viewed his treatment salon as a kind of glorified massage parlor, where Mesmer and his young attractive male assistant magnetizers would produce marvelous and miraculous cures of the courtly women who flocked there. There were jealous husbands. There were also scientists who doubted the validity of the theories upon which Mesmer based his practice.

In 1784, France's King Louis XVI appointed a total of nine commissioners from the Royal Academy of Science to investigate Mesmer's theory and practice. Included among them was the physician Joseph Guillotine, who, after the French Revolution, became famous for his invention of what was supposed to be a more humane method of execution. Also on the commission was Benjamin Franklin, who at the time was the American ambassador to France and also a renowned scientist. You may recall that Ben Franklin flew his famous kite and demonstrated that lightning was actually electricity. The fact that such an obvious observation needed confirmation is evidence of the large amount of yet undiscovered knowledge about electromagnetic science.

The commission focused primarily upon Mesmer's assertion that he had discovered that the human body contains magnetic fluid. The commission found no evidence for such a fluid and therefore rejected his theory and the medical practice based upon it. Mesmer was essentially put out of business.

Still, some form of a belief in the healing power of magnets survives even today. In stores and on the internet you can buy all kinds of magnetic products including bracelets, shoes and belts among many other items. One website claims that an estimated 140 million people worldwide use magnetic therapy to relieve pain, improve circulation, reduce swelling, minimize stiffness, and generally improve the quality of life.

Mesmerism Lived On as a Form of Entertainment

Mesmerism and animal magnetism did not die but simply went underground or morphed into other forms. Just as many people in the general population were undaunted by the Enlightenment's debunking of Father Gassner's activities, so were many people unconvinced by the evidence disproving Mesmer's dramatic results. So, during the last part of the 1700s and the early 1800s, there were many practicing Mesmerists who, calling themselves animal magnetizers, put on a fine show. Many of them were traveling Mesmerists who went from village to village in their wagons selling medicinal potions, putting on a magic show, often with the climax being a dramatic demonstration of the power of animal magnetism.

The practitioner would ask for volunteers from the audience to come up and be magnetized. The show often resembled the kind of performance of contemporary stage hypnotists. Once mesmerized, willing subjects would run around like a chicken or quack like a duck or have hallucinations in which they would be frightened by a ghost. The grand finale often involved the anesthesia of a hand, wherein the subject would be completely numb and the Mesmerist would demonstrate this by passing a needle through the flesh between the thumb and first finger. The mesmerized volunteer would show a complete lack of pain.

An especially famous such traveling showman was Charles Lafontaine. He put on a demonstration in November 1841 in Manchester, England, where the Scottish physician and surgeon James Braid was living. As a source of entertainment, Braid accompanied a friend to the show. His friend, it turned out, became a volunteer, and Braid became convinced of the authenticity of the demonstration, though as an educated physician he knew that magnetic theory had been discredited. He became intrigued about what exactly was going on and began to investigate the phenomenon.

Braid's interest was not just theoretical. As a surgeon, he saw the potential usefulness of the anesthesia created. These were the days before the availability of any chemical anesthetics. The only known way to produce some insensitivity to pain was through the use of alcohol. One can imagine that, before the surgery began, the patient would be given a couple of gulps and maybe one for the surgeon as well to deal with all the screaming.

Mesmerism Newly Understood

In trying to understand what was happening, Braid happened upon the writings of the Marquis de Puysegur, an aristocratic and intellectually curious man who was an officer in the French revolutionary army. He had reformulated the understanding of mesmerism, although his theories were not widely known. He believed that the effects of mesmerism were not due to magnetic influence but instead were the result of what he called the psychic influence of the mesmerist upon the mesmerized subject. He referred to the phenomenon as artificial somnambulism, which roughly means artificial sleep.

Dr. Braid later became acquainted with the work of James Esdaile, also a Scotsman and a physician who published his 1846 book, *Mesmerism*, in India. Dr. Esdaile stumbled upon his own technique of creating surgical anesthesia while practicing in Calcutta, India with the East India Company. At the time, there was an epidemic in Calcutta of scrotal tumors caused by a parasite. The Scottish physician was very troubled by the extreme pain experienced by patients during attempts at surgery to remove these tumors. He believed the mortality rate of over 35 percent during or after such procedures was due to the excruciating pain, leading to shock and the demoralization of the patient. He had never been trained as a mesmerist, nor had he even observed the procedure. But he had heard that Mesmerism could prove useful. So he developed his own technique, which was arduous and involved passing the hands just above the body of a patient for hours at a time to induce a magnetic trance.

Dr. Esdaile soon became exhausted, since his health was rather frail anyway, and decided to delegate the procedure to his native assistants. So, prior to the surgery, during the surgery and during the early hours of recovery, patients were kept in a magnetic trance. The mortality rate dropped from 35 percent to under 5 percent, and the doctor performed hundreds of surgeries using this procedure. He found that a little under a third of his mesmerized patients experienced little or no pain during surgery. For another third, the results were moderate. The remaining patients received only a little benefit.

Hypnosis as the New Way

Back in the latter part of the 1700s, when Mesmer had developed his theories and practices, his work was intended to be based on a scientific view of the human body. Mesmer viewed himself as a reputable member of the scientific community of the Enlightenment. His theory that there was a magnetic body humor turned out to be false but it was not an unreasonable supposition. After all, the science of magnetism and its relationship to electricity was in its infancy. The powerful invisible forces observed in magnets and electrical currents were awe-inspiring and rather baffling to Mesmer's contemporaries.

During this period, the scientific community showed the exuberance of youth, with a proneness to error, as well as dramatic leaps into discovery. It was in this atmosphere that Mesmer put together observations from electromagnetic theory, astrology, oriental medicine, and faith healing and came up with his theory.

His theory, of course, soon became discredited so that by the early 1800s animal magnetism theory and practice had come under the influence of psychics and other occult practitioners. Many varied and wild claims were made about the power of a strong magnetizer. Some believed that such a person could take control of another person's mind and soul, rendering the subject helpless to resist the commands of the animal magnetizer.

James Esdaile came to be a believer in such powers resulting from mesmerism. In some of his writings, he also made extravagant claims regarding the alleged supernatural abilities displayed by patients themselves while under the control of an animal magnetist. In spite of scientific evidence to the contrary, Esdaile remained a believer in the power of magnetic theory to account for his results.

James Braid, on the other hand, was strongly opposed to magnetic theory and coined the term neurohypnology, or neurohypnosis, to explain what was going on with his patients and with those supposedly mesmerized by animal magnetizers. Dr. Braid's new term literally means "nervous sleep" or "sleep of the nerves." He believed that through a process of inducing intense concentration, focus and expectation a person would fall into this special state of sleep. In this state, all of the phenomena characteristic of being mesmerized would occur.

Braid further believed that it was not any special power or animal magnetic power of the operator that led to the results. Instead, it was all a matter of the subject having his imagination and faith captured by the practitioner and then, through a process of monotonous repetition, being lulled to sleep in a special way. In his later writings, Braid dropped the idea that hypnosis was a sleep state. He decided that it was instead a special mental state induced by concentration on a single idea or physical object.

James Braid was the first modern hypnotist. And his understanding of what it involved would stand up even by today's standards. He passionately attempted to render his practices and findings acceptable to the scientific community. So, in a sense, Braid eventually achieved the scientific credibility that Mesmer had sought.

It is clear that the state of mind that Braid and his colleagues were inducing in their patients was essentially the same state of mind that both Father Gassner and Anton Mesmer had induced in their followers seven decades earlier. It is also clear that his way of understanding and utilizing the phenomenon was radically different.

First, although the field of psychology as a separate discipline would not be established for another 40 years, Braid's explanation of hypnotism was psychological in nature. He referred to his patients as being in a special mental state induced by concentration and expectation. This explanation is a far cry from either Gassner's spiritual miracles or Mesmer's magnetically induced healings.

A second difference between Braid and his predecessors was his much more modest claims regarding the benefits of hypnotism. He did not view hypnotism as an alternative to standard medical remedies and procedures. He scoffed at those who claimed that hypnotism or mesmerism was a cure-all. He labeled such people as either naïve or as charlatans. Instead, he was a proponent of the use of hypnotism as an addition to other treatments, either to improve mental attitude or to reduce or eliminate pain while standard therapeutic techniques were being utilized.

Although Braid and Esdaile disagreed regarding the foundations of their work, they were allies in demonstrating the power of their procedures for the relief of pain, especially during surgery. There were other surgeons and physicians who joined their ranks and, by the time Braid and Esdaile had published their works in the mid-1840s, their practices had become widespread in the medical community in Europe and the United States. Hypnotism became widely known and might very well have continued to be the major treatment for severe pain had it not been for a new kind of revolution in anesthesia, namely chemical anesthetics.

The Dawning of the Age of Chemical Anesthesia

A colorful pioneer and tragic figure in this field was the American dentist Horace Wells, who, along with a number of physicians at Massachusetts General Hospital, became convinced of the usefulness of substances such as chloroform, ether and nitrous oxide. Wells himself underwent a surgical procedure while anesthetized with chloroform. He decided, however, that nitrous oxide was more effective and planned a demonstration of the extraction of the tooth of one of his patients before a crowd at the hospital. Apparently, during the procedure the nitrous oxide was improperly mixed with oxygen and when Dr. Wells attempted the extraction the patient cried out in pain, whereupon the crowd began to taunt and jeer and essentially drove Wells off the stage. Wells, it turns out, was a sensitive personality, and the incident so traumatized him that he gave up his career as a dentist and became a traveling salesman for two years in Connecticut and Massachusetts.

After that, Dr. Wells traveled to Paris for a few months where he was reinforced in his ideas. He returned to the United States and sometime during 1848 was able to perform a successful anesthesia of a dental patient before an audience in Philadelphia. However, by the end of that year he had become addicted to chloroform. As his use of the drug became regular, he began to suffer from delusions and hallucinations which culminated in him throwing sulfuric acid at a prostitute on the streets of New York City. He was committed to an insane asylum in lower Manhattan, where he recovered lucidity as the drug wore off. He became so despondent and guilty about what he had done that he committed suicide upon his release, severing an artery in his leg while being partially anesthetized with, you guessed it, chloroform.

Though Horace Wells met a tragic end, the chemical anesthetic movement he advocated rapidly prospered and took hold in the medical establishment. Although death due to overdose of these chemicals began to appear in medical journals, their popularity increased rapidly during the next 20 years or so and, of course, the use of chemical anesthesia during surgery is standard operating procedure to this day.

So, chemical anesthesia crowded out mesmerism or hypnotism as the preferred way of relieving pain during surgery. The reasons for this victory were several. First, the results of administering a chemical anesthetic are consistent and reliable across patients as opposed to the hit-and-miss success rates of magnetism and hypnotism. Also, doctors used to the biological model of medicine were much more comfortable with a chemical effect than with the rather esoteric and baffling results of hypnotic procedures. So, following the adoption of chemical anesthesia for the treatment of pain, mesmerism and hypnosis fell into obscurity for several decades.

Hypnosis as a Tool in the Treatment of Mental Illness

Later in the 1800s, some psychiatrists in France began to use hypnosis as part of their treatment of inmates in an insane asylum. They discovered that certain mental illnesses could be temporarily improved under hypnosis. They also discovered that normal people under hypnosis sometimes display symptoms that resemble mental illness.

It was after visiting this mental hospital and observing the work of psychiatrists there that Sigmund Freud began to develop his theory of the unconscious mind.

Freud was completely blown away when one of the patients who was suffering from a paralysis from the waist down, not only was able to stand and walk while hypnotized but was also able to talk about why the symptom existed. The patient also remembered forgotten memories that had led to the disorder. Then, upon coming out of hypnosis, the patient returned to a paralyzed state and was unable to remember anything that happened under hypnosis, including the memories that had temporarily been restored.

Freud returned to Vienna, where he began to use hypnosis with his own patients and, along with a colleague, had similar dramatic results. One woman patient for instance, was unable to swallow any food and was slowly wasting away. Under hypnosis, she was not only able to eat but talked about the causes of her disorder. And, again in this example, upon awakening she was unable to remember her explanation and returned to her pre-hypnosis condition. Freud later gave up using hypnosis but still recognized its power in certain situations.

So how is it possible that during this altered state of consciousness called hypnosis a person will understand things and remember things that are not understood or remembered during ordinary waking consciousness? The answer is that there is something about hypnosis that enables a person to tap into information from the unconscious mind. So dreams are one way that the unconscious mind communicates with us, and hypnosis is a second way we can open a channel of communication with this deep part of ourselves

When Freud gave up using hypnosis, so did most of his followers so that, yet again, hypnosis fell into disuse.

But just as mesmerism became a source of entertainment long after it was no longer used in medical practice, stage hypnosis is still a popular form of entertainment.

A Revival of the Use of Hypnosis to Control Pain

During both the first and second world wars, there were times when chemical anesthetics were unavailable to help people in pain or in need of surgery. Publications following both wars recounted yet again the powerful anesthetic effects of hypnosis.

In the years following World War II, the use of hypnosis in a variety of contexts became much more prevalent. In addition, hypnosis gained in reputation, and a number of professional journals were established in which hypnosis theory and practice were documented. Since that time, hypnosis has gained in stature and is now practiced by professionals in a variety of fields.

The effectiveness of hypnosis in the relief of pain has always been one of its most widely accepted uses. Research has confirmed the early findings of James Braid and the rest that hypnosis works to reduce and sometimes eliminate pain, even in childbirth.

Hypnosis has also been used by physicians, and by hypnotists working with physicians, to gain control over troublesome behaviors such as smoking or overeating.

In working with patients to deal with pain, or to overcome habits like smoking or overeating, it is now accepted practice to teach patients how to hypnotize themselves. Self-hypnosis provides several advantages over just using hypnosis alone. In the case of pain control, for instance, it is all well and good for a sufferer to experience relief from pain while under hypnosis. But such temporary relief is unlikely to be especially useful for a person suffering from ongoing severe pain, such as in the later stages of cancer.

Having experienced pain relief with a hypnotist does provide the patient with hope. But in order for such relief to be useful, it must continue after the visit is over and the patient has left the hypnotist's office. This is where self-hypnosis comes in.

In the case of overcoming bad habits, the hypnotist's main weapon is the use of what are called post-hypnotic suggestions. For instance, to help a hypnotized person quit smoking, the hypnotist might suggest that in the days ahead cigarette smoke will smell and taste terrible. Such a post-hypnotic suggestion may work for a while but is likely to fade with time. Self-hypnosis provides a means of prolonging the post-hypnotic suggestion indefinitely.

In later chapters, I will present techniques of self-hypnosis for you to use for a number of purposes. In the next chapter, we will begin our exploration of self-hypnosis with a little history.

Chapter 4

Early Self-Hypnosis

As you know, James Braid was the first person to use the term hypnosis. Sometime later, in September 1844, he experienced an attack of rheumatism that he described as so severe that he couldn't take a deep breath without experiencing excruciating pain.

He decided to try to use on himself the techniques that he had successfully used with his patients. He was so unsure of how his experiment in self-hypnosis would work that he asked two friends to observe him during his induction and wake him in case he could not wake himself. He was not at all confident that he would be able to achieve pain relief using his procedure, but he decided to give it a try. By his own account, he was amazed with the results. From this one session of self-hypnosis – which was induced through a procedure of concentrating on a single spot – he said he remained pain-free for over six years.

Later, other physicians taught the technique, which they called auto-suggestion, with excellent success.

For thousands of years, practitioners of one form of meditation or another have also achieved dramatic results. Disciples of meditation – practicing within the context of all the world's major religions – have reported many benefits from their practice. Among these are such things as being totally insensitive to pain or cold or extended periods of fasting.

Contemporary researchers have validated the claims of meditation practitioners who claim they can reduce oxygen consumption, raise and lower the temperature of hands and feet, and achieve other measurable results through the use of meditation.

You might ask whether meditation and self-hypnosis are the same thing. The answer is that they are the same thing called by different names and produced in the context of different kinds of faith or beliefs. Just as mesmerism and hypnosis turned out to be essentially the same thing, the same is probably true of meditation and self-hypnosis.

A second question you might ask is whether or not self-hypnosis can be as effective as the ordinary hypnosis produced when a hypnotist works with a subject. The answer may surprise you. There is no essential difference between the two, except that it is more difficult to give oneself the elaborate post-hypnotic suggestions that are possible with a hypnotist. But, except for that issue, it is safe to say that all hypnosis is self-hypnosis. Hypnosis and self-hypnosis are achieved through a focused concentration on one thought, idea, sight or sound, or a combination of these. In the case of regular hypnosis, the hypnotist provides the object of concentration, usually his own voice. In the case of self-hypnosis, the person himself provides the object upon which to concentrate.

Chapter 5

The Power of the Unconscious Mind

Before we begin to learn self-hypnosis techniques, it would be good to review why this is such an effective tool. What are the benefits that result from using self-hypnosis?

First, self-hypnosis is a way to achieve specific post-hypnotic results like pain relief or to change bad habits such as smoking or overeating.

A second benefit is to quiet the almost endless chatter of the conscious mind in order to make room for the creative healing power of the unconscious mind. Often, the conscious mind and our busy lives make it difficult for us to listen to our inner wisdom.

Another benefit is to open a pathway between the conscious mind and the unconscious mind. During much of our waking life, these two parts of us are mostly cut off from one another. Self-hypnosis is an effective way to bridge that gap.

This third benefit is especially valuable when used to increase the effectiveness of working with dreams. Dreaming, like hypnosis, opens a window between the conscious and the unconscious. Self-hypnosis can help us to take full advantage of that opportunity.

As we will discuss later, self-hypnosis can improve the recall of dreams and in other ways help us to uncover and understand their language and meaning. The pouring forth of the wisdom of the unconscious into the conscious mind is responsible for many of the great creative achievements of humankind. It is also through tapping into the unconscious mind and its healing power that much psychotherapy and other healing practices do their work.

Different Levels of Consciousness

Carl Jung was a Swiss psychiatrist who took many of Sigmund Freud's ideas and developed them in his own way. According to his thinking, the mind can be thought of as divided into three parts: the conscious, the personal unconscious and the collective unconscious. Let's discuss each of these in turn.

As you are reading these words, you are aware of what you're doing and the thoughts that you're thinking as you are processing the information. You may take a break in a few minutes and, while looking out the window, notice a neighbor walking his dog and remember a conversation you recently had with him about dog obedience school. Or you may start to feel hungry and remember that there is some leftover pizza in the refrigerator. All of this kind of information that moves easily in and out of your mind is part of the conscious mind. There is a large storehouse of information in your conscious mind. Of course, not all of it is passing through your awareness at any given moment, but all of it is available as needed.

Some new information is constantly being added to the system, while older or rarely used information will gradually decay and become more difficult, or even impossible, to access. But overall, the conscious mind is pretty stable over time. As we go through our daily lives, we are generally only aware of the conscious mind. That's why it's called the conscious mind.

As for the unconscious mind, many people find the idea of there being things in the mind of which we are unaware to be ridiculous. How could there be something in your mind and you not know about it? Well, let's see if we can make some sense out of the idea of the unconscious mind. We'll start with the personal unconscious.

We have all met people who are very optimistic and always look on the bright side of things. We also have met people who, on a sunny day, expect dark clouds to appear at any moment. Where did these attitudes and feelings come from?

We know from extensive research in the branch of psychology called human development that these differing world views often have their roots in early childhood experiences.

Let's say that you were born into a troubled family. Maybe, during your first year or so of life, your parents were going through a turbulent divorce. Maybe dad had moved out of the house and mother, in her painful state of mind, began to drink alcohol heavily. There you were, a helpless infant totally dependent on the adults around you for care and comfort. But, under the circumstances, you may not have received very good care at all. Perhaps your cries in the middle of the night went unanswered because mother was too intoxicated or tired to respond. You were not held, rocked or comforted much. When you were fed, or your diaper was changed, it was done with few smiles and little conversation.

You weren't yet able to put your reactions into words, but we know that a child does draw some conclusions about the world from these early experiences. If you did have the words, you might have said, "The world is not a very friendly place. There is a lot of pain and loneliness here. Things don't turn out the way I would like them to. In fact, usually things go from bad to worse."

On the other hand, if you were fortunate enough to be raised by loving parents, you also developed an early idea of what the world is like. You might have thought, "Life is really all right. I think I'll stick around. When things get painful or scary, someone comes and makes it all better. There are lots of laughs. Things usually turn out just fine."

The conscious mind has long since forgotten all of those early experiences. But they are permanently lodged in the personal unconscious mind. And those memories have a profound effect upon your adult personality.

There are plenty of "forgotten" childhood memories that continue to influence us. Your adult attitudes toward authority, toward your body, toward pleasure and pain and toward sexuality are all rooted to some degree in these early experiences.

But there is a second source of material in the personal unconscious. It contains all of the thoughts and feelings that we don't allow into the conscious mind. A brief look at human history, with its wars, brutality and atrocities, reveals that the human race has a dark side.

But how many of us would admit to having such barbaric tendencies? So, without being aware of it, we push such thoughts and urges out of the conscious mind and into the unconscious. Sometimes they pop out during a fit of anger. Or they show up in a dream as a bloody nightmare. At such times, the personal unconscious is revealing a bit of its dark side.

The personal unconscious sometimes reveals itself through psychological complexes. You've probably heard of someone having an inferiority complex or a father complex, or a power complex. What exactly is a complex? It is an unconscious pattern of feelings and thoughts centered on a particular theme. For instance, because of early childhood experiences, I might have developed sensitivity around the idea of inferiority. Maybe I was smaller than my siblings. Maybe I was put down by a parent, so that now, as an adult, I tend to read inferiority issues into situations where they don't really exist. This may show up, for instance, as an intense sensitivity to criticism. Or, because of the complex, I may be unable to stand up for myself even when treated very unfairly.

Most of the time, the personal unconscious mind is just there in the background, not doing us any great harm. But there are times in our lives when developing an awareness of its contents can be a big help. At the very least, such knowledge can enrich our self-understanding. Sometimes, such an understanding can help us transform serious psychological or interpersonal challenges. Later, we will be discussing ways of understanding dreams that can be very helpful in this regard.

The Collective Unconscious

The third part of the mind is the most difficult to wrap your conscious mind around. But coming to understand the mysterious richness of the collective unconscious is worth the effort.

To begin to understand the collective unconscious, consider this. In our mothers' wombs, each of us started out as a pinhead-sized living being. Even when we were that small, our one living cell contained more information than a multiple-volume encyclopedia. All of the information necessary to grow a full human body was already there. The blueprints for creating eyes, arms, kidneys, a heart, are contained in this one single cell. Each of these organs is complex almost beyond belief. Yet the information to fashion such miracles is there in that tiny living being.

This vast library of information did not just appear overnight. It is the result of millions of years of accumulated knowledge from the experiences of our ancestors dating back to the dawn of life on earth. Biologists understand that, through a process of natural selection, useful and valuable characteristics were passed on while less adaptive ones were dropped out of the gene pool. We might call this a process of selective biological memory.

Similarly, the collective unconscious developed in much the same way. It contains the memories of generations past, going back for millions of years. In this case, the memories are psychological and experiential rather than biological or anatomical. Contained within these memories are what are called archetypes, which have been compared to animal instincts.

For example, most birds have built into them an instinctive knowledge of how to build nests. Different kinds of birds are pre-programmed to build different kinds of nests. We might say that a bird has a nest archetype contained within its unconscious mind. The individual bird gathers whatever materials are available and creates the best nest it can consistent with the archetype it has inherited. Individual nests will be different, but they will all be consistent with that particular kind of bird's nest archetype.

An example a little closer to home is the archetype contained within dogs that pre-programs them to respond to a leader or a master. From millions of years of ancestral experience as pack animals, dogs have evolved a strong predisposition to experience their social lives through the lens of a master archetype. So when dogs were domesticated, they brought that archetype with them into their relationships with humans. The presence of this master archetype is one of the reasons dogs are so appealing as human companions. Loyalty and obedience come naturally to dogs. The archetype, however, does not predetermine the exact behavior of a specific dog. All dogs, we might say, are born looking for a leader or a master. But if an adequate leader is not found, the dog will find other, perhaps less admirable, ways of acting out this unconscious longing. It might, for instance, try to become a master itself. It might attempt to dominate or attack other dogs or even its own owners.

Humans, being more complex then birds or dogs, possess a collective unconscious that is loaded with rich and compelling archetypes.

One such archetype whose power most of us have experienced and witnessed is the archetype of lover. For instance, it's amazing how one kind of lover or other shows up in the lives of teenagers. In school, on the school bus, on the playground, or on Facebook, there will be somebody who takes your breath away. Love songs get written; hearts catch on fire and get broken. It's all part of living with and through a powerful archetype.

Of course, when you are in the grip of an archetype, you are unaware that the powerful currents of energy coursing through your arteries have their origins in the millions of repeated experiences of our ancestors dating back to the beginning. You believe that your feelings and experiences are specific to the particular boy or girl, man or woman that you've fallen in love with. It's all about her. Her face, her skin, her perfumed hair, are driving you crazy. But that's only the tip of the iceberg, the surface-level waves that have their origins in the deepest oceans of the collective unconscious.

The archetype can express itself in widely different ways. For instance, for some young women, the beloved may be an imaginary, impossibly idealized man. She may spend hours in front of the mirror putting on makeup, trying on clothes and checking out different facial expressions in order to try to figure out how to best win the heart of this archetypical lover.

For another young woman, who is beginning to feel same-sex attraction, the image of an admired woman teacher may get all tangled up with the beautiful glow-in-the-dark lover archetype. Just being in this teacher's classroom will take the girl's breath away.

For many of us, the lover archetype will lead us into making life-changing decisions like getting married. Once I marry the woman of my dreams and settle down with her, other archetypes may join the chorus. For instance, the mother archetype might kick in and I begin to view my wife through that lens. I might perceive her as scolding me or treating me like a little boy even when she's not. I might even call her my old lady.

The hero is another compelling archetype that has its roots in the common, and repeated, experiences of our ancestors. In families, we often see this archetype showing up as young children worship their older siblings. Kings, emperors and ruthless dictators have exploited this fountainhead of deep unconscious energy. Leaders have sometimes been described as being "bigger than life." How true that is. For the archetype is always more powerful than the individual to whom it is attached. Adolf Hitler burned brightly with archetypical light that was distorted and turned to cruel and inhumane purposes. The mystery of how an entire nation of educated men and women could be caught in the grip of such insanity is at least partly answered through an understanding of the hero archetype.

As these examples illustrate, an archetype is neither good nor bad in and of itself. The archetypes of hero, lover, father, goddess or priest, to name just a few, can bring forth meaning and beauty in life. Under other circumstances, any one of these archetypes can plunge those possessed by them into irrational and destructive caverns of unconsciousness.

Another thing about the vast storehouse of the collective unconscious is that it is the source from which great works of art, creative masterpieces of mythology and lofty mystical and religious ecstasies spring forth.

You may not consider yourself a creative genius, but you and I can gain our own kind of access to the collective unconscious through learning to remember and understand our dreams. Not all dreams tap into these deepest levels of consciousness, but the ones that do can have a profound and healing effect upon the dreamer.

There is a question about the collective unconscious that has come up from time to time in my dream groups and classes over the years. I have heard people in dream groups share dreams that they believed came from their own particular ethnic memories. For instance, an African-American man had over the years recalled dreams in which he was a slave. One repetitive dream was him hiding out and secretly trying to learn how to read. He knew in the dream that, if he was caught, the penalty was death. He reported that these dreams had a special intensity and vividness about them as though they were actual memories.

Similarly, a Jewish woman had as a child been troubled by dreams of persecution. In many of the dreams, she was a child hiding with her family in terror of being detected. As she got older, she recognized her dreams in the stories told to her by her grandparents about the persecution of her ancestors in Russia, Poland and Germany. There have been other dream group members who believe that certain of their dreams are rooted in their particular ethnic background.

Is there any sense in which the concept of the collective unconscious could explain such dream experiences? In his early writings on the collective unconscious, Carl Jung seemed to agree that there are ethnic differences in the contents of the collective unconscious that are accounted for by the different collective experiences of different ethnic groups. In later writings, he seems to have changed his mind and came to believe that the structures and contents of the collective unconscious are universal among all ethnic groups. But that does not necessarily end the conversation. At the very least, I would say that the experience of ethnic memory dreams is pretty common. It would be hard to sort out whether they are bubbling up from the collective unconscious or are a result of family stories and folklore taking root in impressionable young minds. Either way, remembering and appreciating such dreams can enrich a person's sense of identity and belonging in his family of origin. Such an outcome can be very beneficial.

And so, in review, the personal unconscious is a complex storehouse of memories, emotions and longings that have accumulated during your lifetime to this point. It has the power to affect your daily experience of life in profound ways. If you shine the light of self-awareness even more deeply into the recesses of your mind, you will come upon the archetypes of the collective unconscious. Understanding how you have danced to the music of these archetypes and made them your own can be enlightening.

In future discussions we will refer to the personal unconscious and the collective unconscious taken together, as simply the unconscious mind.

Two tools for gaining access to these unconscious realms are dream interpretation and self-hypnosis. In the next chapter, you'll begin to learn some powerful self- hypnosis techniques to accomplish this exciting work.

But is it always a good idea to try to break down the boundary between these two layers of the mind?

War and Peace Between the Conscious and Unconscious Minds

What kinds of communication and how much communication should there be between the conscious and the unconscious minds? Is more communication always desirable?

For most of us, the answer is yes. Not only will we gain insight and self-understanding, but, as we will discuss later, there is a treasure trove of creativity concealed in the deeper levels of our minds.

But what about mental patients? Among mildly disturbed patients, the goal is to increase conscious awareness of what's in the unconscious mind. Things like irrational fears and troubling compulsions can be improved if the sufferer becomes aware of their roots in the unconscious mind.

Among the seriously mentally ill, on the other hand, who are hearing voices or seeing visions, the goal is to strengthen the boundary between the conscious and the unconscious so that the flood of unconscious material into the conscious mind becomes less frightening and destructive.

Whether we're trying to open the window wider or close it down some, it's clear that the mind has a powerful influence on our daily lives. The expression "mind over matter" points to this important truth.

It is obvious that your conscious mind plays a big role in your life. Thoughts you're thinking directly affect what you do and how you feel. If you think your boss is a jerk, that will stimulate angry feelings and may result in nasty behaviors.

There is a method of psychotherapy based on the idea that if you change the way you think you can change the way you feel. This method is called cognitive therapy and has shown itself to be effective in working with people suffering from depression. The idea is simple. Thinking pessimistic and despairing thoughts will lead to painful feelings. On the other hand, happy thoughts will generate happy feelings.

And then there is the influence of the unconscious mind. Sigmund Freud's biggest contribution was the idea that troubling content from the unconscious mind can rise to the surface, affecting thoughts, moods and behavior. This can only lead to trouble.

Psychotherapists who buy this idea argue that trying to change conscious thoughts through cognitive therapy will be a failure unless the unconscious material is dealt with.

For instance, a depressed person may be suffering from unconscious guilt from real or imagined past sins. The conscious mind can think all of the positive thoughts it wants, but the lousy feelings will stay put unless the mess in the unconscious mind is cleaned up.

I have already introduced the idea that hypnosis and dream work can open up channels between these two centers of consciousness. Let's continue to look at some of the ways that this can be valuable.

Sometimes the unconscious mind can pick up information from the outside world that the conscious mind is unaware of. In this sense, the unconscious mind displays more wisdom than the conscious mind. Later we will discuss cases where the unconscious mind already knew that an illness, such as cancer, was developing in the body, long before the conscious mind figured it out.

You'll also learn about scientific and creative breakthroughs that have entered the conscious minds of artists and inventors from the unconscious mind through dreams.

The following example shows that the unconscious mind can sometimes have a better handle on what's good for a person than the conscious mind does.

Jack came to me for hypnosis. He was in his third year of medical school when he began to develop a phobia about driving or riding in a car. Since this was the only form of transportation back and forth to medical school, the phobia was threatening his academic career.

The situation could be looked at like this: his conscious mind wanted him to continue studying to be a physician. But his unconscious mind held an opposite second opinion. The unconscious mind was bound and determined to sabotage his conscious intentions. And the more he pushed back and tried to overcome the phobia, the worse things got. He wanted me to use hypnosis to overcome this career-threatening fear.

I asked him if there was any reason to think that his decision to attend medical school was not what he truly wanted to do. He was shocked by the question and nearly stormed out of my office. After he calmed down I pointed out that his very reaction might suggest that I had asked the right question.

He reluctantly agreed that the hypnosis session would not be about forcing him to overcome his phobia, at least not at first. Instead, it would be used to check out the possibility that there was an internal conflict about whether or not medical school was the right thing to be doing with his life.

Jack arrived at our next session relieved that the phobia had decreased in intensity. At the same time, he was distressed by a nightmare that had been repeated three times that week. I explained that dreams are a major way for the unconscious mind to tell its side of the story. Here is the dream.

He was performing surgery on a patient. At some point, he became aware that he was operating on himself. He was both the surgeon and the patient. As the surgery continued, he started making mistakes. At one point, he nicked an artery and the bleeding was so severe that the teaching surgeon he was working with had to take over to save the patient's life.

The same dream repeated itself three nights in a row. Each night the situation got worse. The third night, he woke up unsure of whether or not he had survived.

As a result of this dream, a whole flood of insights bubbled up to the surface of Jack's mind. His big realization was that medical school was not really the choice of his heart. Both his father and his grandfather had been physicians and he had been groomed from early childhood to follow in their footsteps. His conscious mind was on board with this decision, but at a deeper level there was rebellion. The dream convinced him that if he continued on this course it could very well kill him or at least, as he put it, kill his soul. This is an example of when the conscious mind really needs to listen to the wisdom of the unconscious mind.

But sometimes the unconscious mind can get stuck and need the encouragement and soothing of the conscious mind. As we will discover later, post-traumatic stress disorder provides an example of how this can happen. A person with PTSD is often haunted by memories from years or even decades earlier. Nightmares, flashbacks and awful feelings of anxiety and dread can dominate the person's life. The conscious mind knows that these memories are from the distant past and are best left there. But the unconscious mind seems determined to keep them alive, to the detriment of the sufferer.

In cases such as these, self-hypnosis, meditation and guided imagery would help in the work of healing the wounds that are lodged in the unconscious mind. In this way, the conscious mind, which in this situation is being more realistic, can positively influence the unconscious mind.

It is essential to gain access to the unconscious mind whether the goal is to learn from it or to influence it in positive ways. In the next chapter, you'll learn a number of self- hypnosis techniques to accomplish this important work.

Chapter 6

Self-Hypnosis

In this chapter, I will be presenting two self-hypnosis techniques for you to practice. In the next chapter, you'll learn a third.

The first is a daytime self-hypnosis. The second is a bedtime technique that takes advantage of the borderline state between being awake and being asleep.

In daytime self-hypnosis, you will be setting aside a brief period of time to practice self-hypnosis and self-suggestion. For anyone who has practiced meditation, this procedure will be familiar.

The best way to proceed with this first kind of self-hypnosis is to prepare a recording of the hypnotic inductions that I will be sharing with you. Using your own voice usually is very effective because your mind and your voice already tend to be in harmony from years of familiarity with each other. But if for some reason you are uncomfortable listening to your own voice and have unsuccessfully tried to get used to it, ask someone else to do the recording for you.

My website, www.hypnosisdreams.com, also offers recordings I have prepared of all of these scripts. Many people find these professionally prepared recordings to be most effective.

Before we get started, I want to tell you some things about how we experience the world around us that will make a big difference in your success in using self-hypnosis.

Our Senses

Seeing is believing. Or maybe hearing is believing. Or maybe touching is believing. The truth is that it seems to depend upon the individual which of these statements is closest to the truth. For some of us, the world is a visual playground full of all kinds of sights to feast our eyes on. For others, the world is full of sounds. Still others seem to feel their way through their days.

Of course, if our sensory equipment is working properly, we use all three kinds of ways of being in the world. But the interesting thing is that most of us have a favorite channel of experience. To get the most out of your self-hypnosis work, it would be a good idea to figure out which kind of person you are.

One way to start figuring this out is to focus on how you experience the world around you when things are calm and not much is going on. At such times, notice what you're experiencing. While you're taking a walk, do you tend to be aware of what your eyes are seeing? Do you notice colors, lightness, darkness, contrasts, and so on? Or are you more aware of the sounds going on around you? Do you notice the sound of the wind in the trees or traffic nearby or the sounds of birds? Or are you more aware of things like the warmth of the sun on your skin, the breeze against your face or the feel of the ground beneath your feet?

What you'll find as you become more aware of this kind of thing is that it's a pretty mixed bag. But you may notice that one of these ways of experiencing the world is a little more dominant than the other two.

Another way of pinning this down is to listen to the words you choose to express yourself. To get a sense of what I mean, read the following three paragraphs and see if you can notice a difference that reflects how each of these three people experiences the world.

"I can't seem to get a clear picture of what you are talking about. I can see that you're unhappy and it looks like you're going to end your marriage, but I still don't see why. I guess you and your wife don't see eye to eye . She is a colorful personality, but she's bright and there probably is never a dull moment."

"When you say you want to quit your job, I hear you loud and clear. I've tried to listen to your complaints but you've been so quiet. I want to tell you that it's time to speak up and not just quietly walk away. You are intelligent and we need your voice to be heard in this organization."

"I feel that we have hit a rough spot in our relationship. Let's try to get a handle on what went wrong and see if we can come to grips with the real issues. I know that these are hard issues to tackle, but if we can each soften our positions we can get somewhere. I would really like to rekindle the fire that used to keep our relationship interesting."

You might want to say that people don't really talk this way. And you'd be right. These three paragraphs are full of figures of speech and are designed to show the contrast among the three ways of experiencing the world. In case it's not already clear, the first paragraph demonstrates a seeing or looking orientation. The second demonstrates a hearing or listening style. And the third paragraph is an example of a person experiencing the world through feeling and touching.

How the Senses Evolve Through Childhood

A question that may arise is which of these three is the most important? One answer is that it varies from person to person, as we have just described. But another approach is to ask in what order these styles develop during childhood.

Just take a look at a baby or toddler and you can see that the sense of touch is very important. In fact, during the first months of life, seeing and hearing are not much in evidence. The young person feels his way through his days. Nursing, being held, soiling his diaper and so on, all involve touching and feeling. Softness, warmth, hunger, discomfort and pain all are touch and feel activities. A little later, as the child begins to explore his world, touching continues to be primary. Seeing is not enough. As any parent knows, children of this age seem to want to touch everything. Telling the child to look but not touch is an almost unnatural command. It's as though things are not real to the child until they are touched.

Then there is the Bible story of Doubting Thomas, who would not believe that Jesus was resurrected even when he saw him with his own eyes. The story tells us that he actually had to touch Jesus' wounds in order to believe that it was truly his Lord. This story reflects our sense that touching something is a more powerful kind of proof than just seeing it.

Hearing and listening seems to be the second system to develop. Loud noises will startle a newborn baby and the sound of mother's voice is recognized very early.

Seeing and looking also starts early but have to wait for the eyes to develop before much precision is achieved in looking at things. But infants can certainly be observed in deep concentrated gazing at mother's face very early in life.

So what does all of this have to do with dreaming and hypnosis? The first thing to say is that, for just about everybody, looking and seeing are the primary experiences during dreaming. Other senses sometimes kick in, as in hearing a voice, feeling a touch, or smelling an aroma. But these experiences are almost always secondary to the visual intensity of dreams. This is true even among people who are otherwise listeners or feelers. So there seems to be a transition in favor of seeing as we go to sleep and begin to dream. That the eyes are the primary sense organ during dreaming is also indicated by the very name of dream sleep. As we will discuss later, rapid eye movement sleep is the stage when dreams occur.

Early in your self-hypnosis practice, induction seems to go more smoothly when the words used are matched with your primary way of sensing the world. Later on, it doesn't make very much of a difference

It is best for your first hypnosis experience, to use a script tailored to your primary sensory preference. In this way, you quickly strengthen your ability to go into hypnosis. Once you have achieved some hypnosis practice, you can then move on to applying what you've learned to specific goals, such as improved dream recall, getting a better night's sleep or quitting smoking, among many other possibilities. These later scripts need not be tailored to your sensory preference.

Recordings I have prepared for you to use for many self-improvement projects are available on my website, www.hypnosisdreams.com.

So now you are ready to use recorded scripts to take yourself into a deep and relaxing level of self-hypnosis.

The first script is for those who haven't been able to decide which sensory modality is dominant or if you've come to think that you use a mixture of all three.

A Script for a Person with a Mixed or Undetermined Sensory Preference

As we begin, allow your eyes to comfortably close and feel your body settling down into a state of increasing relaxation. You'll begin to notice your breathing, steady and rhythmic. Focus on your breathing for a moment. Feel your chest and stomach area rising and falling with each breath. As you are monitoring your breathing, you'll notice your mind becoming more focused on the sound of my voice. Feel the sound of my voice relaxing you. My voice seems to enter into your inner mind and bring you peace.

You can feel your body relaxing more and more. Now follow along with me as I take you on a tour of your ever more relaxed body. Feel your forehead and scalp letting go of all tension and tightness. Feel your face relaxing the muscles and nerves behind your eyes, behind your cheeks, behind your nose. All tension is melting away. You can feel the inside of your mouth letting go of any tension and any tightness.

Notice the relaxation spreading down from your cheeks and chin and jaw into your neck and throat, relaxing more and more. Feel the mechanism for swallowing relaxing; the mechanism for speech relaxing; your throat, your neck and shoulders relaxing; your arms, your upper arms relaxing, then down to your elbows; feel your forearms, your wrists, your hands, your fingers right down to your fingertips completely relax. Feel the relaxation, feel the letting go, letting go more and more.

You can picture yourself lying back and relaxing. It's a beautifully comforting picture. You're surrounded by a natural, warm glowing light that brings you comfort, warmth and color.

You continue to feel relaxed down into your abdominal area and into your pelvic area, your hips. The very center of your being is relaxing, and all tension is melting away. Now down to your thighs and knees, your lower legs, and ankles and feet completely relaxed, letting go, relaxing, letting go.

To deepen you further in this state, I want you to imagine that you're lying back on a beautiful beach. You're perfectly at ease on the beach. It's quiet but you can hear the rhythmic movement of waves. You can hear the breeze passing through some grass. Perhaps the breeze is stirring some palm trees nearby. You can feel the cool breeze on your face, and you can feel the warm sun warming your face so that there is a perfect balance between the cool breeze and the warm sun, so that you feel contained within perfection.

As you lie back on the beach, you look out across the ocean and see the sun sparkling off the waves -- you see the white caps -- you're aware of how white and beautiful the sand is. You hear the sound of the ocean; you feel the warm sun, the cool breeze; you see the waves and the sand; you see the blue sky up above, with a few white puffy clouds, and you can almost feel yourself drifting with those clouds, moving deeper and deeper into relaxation, all the way down, deeply relaxed, deeply into hypnosis, getting deeper and deeper and deeper and deeper, all the way down.

In order to deepen you even further into a deep level of hypnosis, I'm going to count backwards from 20 down to zero. As I count, I want you to count silently along with me. Don't count out loud or even move your lips; just think each number so that as I say each number, and you think each number, your mind becomes even more fully focused on the sound of my voice, and my voice will take you even deeper into a peaceful place of deep, relaxing and healing hypnosis.

So follow along with me now, counting with me as I count from 20 to 0. You might visualize the numbers as though they were illuminated numbers on a screen passing by in front of you; or you might feel yourself walking down a flight of softly and thickly carpeted stairs, walking down a stair with each number, starting with 20, and as you move down the stairway with each number. So you might picture the numbers, or you might feel yourself moving down the stairway, or you might simply hear my voice taking you down deeper into hypnosis with each number.

Whatever works best for you is fine, or you might move from one idea or image to the other and then settle on the one that works best. But in any case, count silently along with me, follow along with me now, focusing on the sound of my voice, counting with me now, 20, 19, 18, 17, 16, 15, 14, 13, 12, 10, 9, 8, 7,6 ,5, 4, 3, 2, 1, 0.

Now, before I bring you out of this relaxed hypnotic state that you're in right now, we will take a moment more to enjoy this relaxed and peaceful place.

Feel your entire body relaxed and comfortable and at ease. You can still experience the pleasure of the deepening hypnosis that you've achieved through counting from 20 to 0. You're still there on the beautiful beach.

Now I'm going to bring you out of the state of hypnosis by counting from 1 to 5. As I count, you'll feel your arms and hands, legs and feet, becoming lighter; your body beginning to feel less completely relaxed; your mind becoming more focused on the outer world and less deeply engrossed in your imagination and the sound of my voice.

As I count from 1 to 5, you will gradually return to normal, natural waking state until, by the count of 5, you'll be completely wide awake; you'll feel refreshed, relaxed, alert and very, very good; now 1, 2, 3, 4, 5. Wide awake.

A Script for a Person Who is a Hearing or Listening Type

"Sit back, relax and close your eyes. Focus your mind on the sound of my voice. Notice that the sound of my voice enters into your mind and relaxes you more and more. You can feel your mind settling into the hearing of the sound of my voice and relaxing more and more. As you let my voice drift into your mind, you float on my voice like the sound of peaceful harmony and gentle, almost whispering, music. Let yourself drift into a quiet sense of deep relaxation. As you settle back, you may hear sounds in the distance. Those sounds will serve to further relax you. Those sounds are almost like a lullaby, quietly soothing and relaxing you. If you are inside, maybe you can hear the sound of the fan of the air conditioner or heating system. Let those sounds drift into your mind and quietly surround you with relaxation, peace and well-being. You may also hear the sound of distant traffic or the sound of birds or the sound of your own heartbeat in your ears. The rhythmic sounds of your own breathing will serve to further bring you peace and quietly move you deeper into an inner place of rest and relaxation.

As you continue to focus, my voice will take you to an even more peaceful scene. Imagine that you are lying back on a beautiful beach. You're aware of your surroundings. You can hear the rhythmic breaking of the waves against the shore. You can hear the sounds of seagulls in the distance and the sound of a breeze stirring the fronds of some palm trees nearby. You're aware of the warm sun on your body, warming and relaxing you. You can feel the penetrating heat of the sun melting all of your tensions away. As you look around in your minds eye, you can see the white sparkling sand, the deep blue sea, the sun reflecting off the waves. There is a blue sky up above with a few white puffy clouds drifting overhead. You're completely at peace and drifting deeper and deeper into a state of profound relaxation and gradually deepening hypnosis.

In order to deepen you even further into a deep level of hypnosis, I'm going to count backwards from 20 down to 0. As I count, I want you to count silently along with me. Don't count out loud or even move her lips. Just think each number so that as I say each number and you think each number, your mind becomes even more fully focused on the sound of my voice, and my voice will take you even deeper into a peaceful place of deep, relaxing and healing hypnosis.

So follow along with me now, counting with me as I count from 20 to 0. Simply hear my voice taking you down deeper into hypnosis with each number.

Now, count silently along with me. Follow along with me now, focusing on the sound of my voice, counting with me now, 20, 19, 18, 17, 16, 15, 14, 13, 12, 10, 9, 8, 7, 6, 5, 4, 3, 2, 1, 0.

Now, before I bring you out of this relaxed hypnotic state, we will take a moment more to enjoy this relaxed and peaceful place.

Feel your entire body relaxed and comfortable and at ease. You can still experience the pleasure of the deepening hypnosis that you've achieved through counting from 20 to 0. You're still there on the beautiful beach.

Now I'm going to bring you out of the state of hypnosis by counting from 1 to 5. As I count, you'll feel your arms and hands, legs and feet, becoming lighter; your body beginning to feel less completely relaxed; your mind becoming more focused on the outer world and less deeply engrossed in your imagination and the sound of my voice.

As I count from 1 to 5, you will gradually return to a normal, natural, waking state until, by the count of 5, you'll be completely wide awake; you'll feel refreshed, relaxed, alert, and very, very good. Awake.

A Script for People of the Feeling and Touching Type

Close your eyes, sit back and focus on the sound of my voice. Feel my voice seeming to penetrate into your mind and relax you. As you feel my voice capturing your attention and bringing you into a place of peace, feel your body beginning to relax. Feel your scalp muscles relaxing. Feel your face letting go of all tightness as the tension melts away. You feel those sensations of relaxation spreading from your scalp to your face to your neck and throat. It's as though my voice is touching you and massaging away any anxiety or tension. You can feel the sensations of relaxation continuing from your neck to your back and shoulders, arms and hands, legs and feet and abdominal area. All tension and anxiety is melting away, melting away from all parts of your body. You might imagine that you're lying back in a warm bath. You can feel the warmth surrounding and relaxing every part of your body.

To deepen you further, I want you to imagine that you're lying back on a beautiful beach. You can feel the warm sun relaxing you as the sun's rays warm your body. You may feel a slight breeze keeping you pleasantly cool. As the sun warms and the breeze cools you, there is a perfect balance in your sensations, so that you can relax and drift deeper and deeper into hypnosis.

As you lie back on the beach, you're also aware of the white sands around you, and in your mind's eye you can see the beauty and the whiteness of the beach. You look out across the ocean and see the sun's reflection shimmering off the waves. The contrast between the depths of the darkness of the sea and the sun's brightness reflecting off the surface pulls you even deeper into relaxation and into hypnosis. You look up and see the blue sky, and that further relaxes you as you watch a few white puffy clouds drifting overhead. You can almost imagine drifting with those clouds and floating, relaxing even more deeply.

In order to deepen you even further into a deep level of hypnosis, I'm going to count backwards from 20 down to zero. As I count, I want you to count silently along with me. Don't count out loud or even move your lips. Just think each number, so that as I say each number and you think each number, your mind becomes even more fully focused on the sound of my voice, and my voice will take you even deeper into a peaceful place of deep, relaxing and healing hypnosis.

So follow along with me now, counting with me as I count from 20 to 0. Feel yourself walking down a flight of softly and thickly carpeted stairs; walking down a stair with each number, starting with 20.

Count silently along with me now, focusing on the sound of my voice, counting with me now, 20, 19, 18, 17, 16, 15, 14, 13, 12, 10, 9, 8, 7, 6, 5, 4, 3, 2, 1, 0.

Now, before I bring you out of this relaxed hypnotic state that you're in right now, we will take a moment more to enjoy this relaxed and peaceful place.

Feel your entire body relaxed and comfortable and at ease. You can still experience the pleasure of the deepening hypnosis that you've achieved through counting from 20 to 0. You're still there on the beautiful beach.

Now I'm going to bring you out of the state of hypnosis by counting from 1 to 5. As I count, you'll feel your arms and hands, legs and feet, becoming lighter; your body beginning to feel less completely relaxed; your mind becoming more focused on the outer world and less deeply engrossed in your imagination and the sound of my voice.

As I count from 1 to 5, you will gradually return to normal, natural, waking state until by the count of 5 you'll be completely wide awake. You'll feel refreshed, relaxed, alert and very, very good. Now, 1, 2, 3, 4, 5. Wide awake.

A Script for the Seeing Person

Sit back, relax, and focus your mind on my voice. The sound of my voice will soothe and relax you. As you let go of all tension and all tightness, you can picture the tension of your muscles softening and melting away. As you lie back, you can see yourself in your mind's eye being pulled by gravity down into the chair, or the sofa, or the bed. You can feel the muscles in your scalp and face relaxing. There is a soft, gentle, dreamy light around your body, surrounding you with its warmth and peaceful glow. It's as though there is a peaceful and harmonious aura surrounding you and bringing you deeply and profoundly in touch with your inner center of peace. You might imagine that place as being a golden glowing ball at the center of your being. This golden ball is bringing you to an ever-healthier and more relaxing and peaceful state as you continue in this process of deepening hypnosis.

To deepen you even further in this state, I want you to imagine that you're lying back on a beautiful beach. This beach is so beautiful that it seems heavenly, its warmth and glow perfect. You can see the white sands all around you, clean and pure and unspoiled. You can see the sun reflecting off the sand. Nearby, you can see the sea with its deep blue color and the sun's reflection sparkling on the surface. You can see the breaking waves, with whitecaps and churning water bringing you a sense of being part of something greater than yourself. And that brings you more deeply into hypnosis.

In order to deepen you even further into a deep level of hypnosis, I'm going to count backwards from 20 down to 0. As I count, I want you to count silently along with me. Don't count out loud or even move your lips. Just think each number so that as I say each number and you think each number your mind becomes even more fully focused on the sound of my voice, and my voice will take you even deeper into a peaceful place of deep, relaxing and healing hypnosis.

So follow along with me now, counting with me as I count from 20 to 0. Visualize the numbers as though they were illuminated numbers on a screen passing by in front of you.

Count silently along with me now, focusing on the sound of my voice, counting with me now, 20, 19, 18, 17, 16, 15, 14, 13, 12, 10, 9, 8, 7, 6, 5, 4, 3, 2, 1, 0.

Now, before I bring you out of this relaxed hypnotic state that you're in, we will take a moment more to enjoy this relaxed and peaceful place.

Feel your entire body relaxed and comfortable and at ease. You can still experience the pleasure of the deepening hypnosis that you've achieved through counting from 20 to 0. You're still there on the beautiful beach.

Now, I'm going to bring you out of the state of hypnosis by counting from 1 to 5. As I count, you'll feel your arms and hands, legs and feet, becoming lighter; your body beginning to feel less completely relaxed; your mind becoming more focused on the outer world and less deeply engrossed in your imagination and the sound of my voice.

As I count from 1 to 5, you will gradually return to a normal, natural, waking state until, by the count of 5, you'll be completely wide awake. You'll feel refreshed, relaxed, alert and very, very good. Now 1, 2, 3, 4, 5. Wide awake.

Bedtime Self-hypnosis

You have now learned how to take yourself into a self-hypnotic place during the day. I will now teach you how to take advantage of the twilight zone between being awake and being asleep.

You'll not need to record anything in order to do this bedtime self-hypnosis. Instead, just read the following instructions and practice along with me right now. Because you will be practicing this technique now, make sure that you are currently in a situation where you can relax and not be distracted for about 10 minutes. Practicing this technique will take you into your own inner world, so make sure you're in a safe and comfortable place. Read and practice the following instructions a few times and you'll be set to use the technique at bedtime.

Alternately you can go to my website, www.hypnosisdreams.com and order a recording that will take you through the entire process.

After you've settled down into bed and are in the comfortable position in which you normally go to sleep, I want you to repeat a phrase 20 times. I'll describe the exact nature of that phrase in a moment, but first I want to describe for you how you will proceed to repeat the phrase 20 times.

In order to keep track of how many times you've said the phrase, and to push the phrase deeply into your unconscious mind, I want you to press down ever so slightly with each finger on each hand in turn, going through each hand twice for a total of 20 times.

So you start with the thumb on your left hand and press and say the phrase. Now, when you say the phrase, don't say it out loud. Don't even move your lips. Just think the phrase in your mind. And as you press down with your fingers, don't exert very much pressure at all.

Just move your fingers ever so slightly, just enough pressure to keep track of where you are in the sequence of repeating the phrase 20 times.

You can use this technique to give yourself any positive post-hypnotic suggestion. For now, let's use a general positive suggestion that promotes two things that most of us want more of. The phrase is: "I'm feeling more relaxed and confident every day."

Follow along with me in your mind and with your fingers as we practice this procedure which you'll use at bedtime. As you read the following words, follow along with your fingers and imagine that you're lying in bed practicing this technique of self-hypnosis. Then, tonight, you will begin using it regularly.

Again, follow along with me, pressing each finger in turn starting with the thumb of your left-hand. Press and think: *"I'm feeling more relaxed and confident everyday."* Then the first finger: *"I'm feeling more relaxed and confident everyday."* Then the middle finger: *"I'm feeling more relaxed and confident everyday."* Ring finger: *"I'm feeling more relaxed and confident everyday."* Pinky: *"I'm feeling more relaxed and confident everyday."* Then move on to your right hand and do it again. Return to your left-hand and then on to your right-hand once again for a total of 20 times.

And that's all there is to it. You just move through each hand twice, pressing with your fingers ever so slightly as you think the phrase, following along with each press of your fingers. This process will move the phrase gradually down into the space between your conscious and unconscious mind. The transition between being awake and being asleep is a perfect window through which to enter helpful and creative information into that space. In this case, that information will lead to increased feelings of relaxation and confidence.

If after 20 repetitions of the phrase you're still awake, you could start over and repeat the phrase another 20 times. On the other hand, you may drift off to sleep before you've even finished the first 20 repetitions of the phrase. That would be just fine. The words will drift into the space between your conscious and your unconscious mind as you drift off to sleep.

A recording of this entire self hypnosis technique is available on my website, www.hypnosisdreams.com.

In the next chapter, you'll learn to use storytelling as a form of self-hypnosis. This can be a very effective way of giving yourself post-hypnotic suggestions.

Chapter 7

Storytelling

In chapter 6, you learned two self-hypnosis techniques. In the first, you were taught how to construct a script to enter deeply into a quiet hypnotic place. In the second technique, you learned how to practice repeating a post-hypnotic suggestion to yourself just before going to sleep at night. Bedtime is a perfect time to practice self-hypnosis since you are in transition between being awake and being asleep. This twilight zone opens a window for you into the space between your conscious and your unconscious mind.

Storytelling is a form of self-hypnosis that uses indirect suggestions. We receive indirect suggestions from the outside world all the time. Advertisers use this technique a lot. The message may be subtle, or maybe not so subtle, that if you use their product, it will bring you happiness, success, or a beautiful and desirable partner.

Telling a good story can have a significant effect upon the listener. The story of the crucifixion and resurrection of Christ has sometimes been referred to as the greatest story ever told. Gripping and dramatic stories lie at the center of all of the great religions of the world. It goes without saying that these stories have had profound and life-changing effects upon people. On a more mundane level, stories told in families, among friends, and in psychotherapy can have significant effects as well. Attitudes and behaviors can shift dramatically as a result of stories that touch the heart, or, as we might say, the unconscious mind.

Consider the following brief story about the much-hated man who held the last Russian tsarina under his spell. It's a story that I told to James, a patient at a community mental health center:

"It's more difficult to kill somebody than most people think. My favorite example of this is the story of the Russian mystic, Grigori Rasputin, who died in 1916 of hypothermia after he was thrown through the ice into a frigid river. This homicidal

act was apparently an attempt to finish him off after his killers had poisoned him; shot him four times, including one shot to the head; and bludgeoned him. The guy just would not give up the ghost. The challenging nature of the task of snuffing out a life is also made clear by the fact that the majority of suicide attempts end in frustration."

This brief story served as an indirect post-hypnotic suggestion to one of my clients who had begun to talk about committing suicide. If you read this paragraph as just a story, you would miss the fact that there are a lot of suggestions embedded in it.

The first message, which is just below the surface, is that bringing about death, either one's own or somebody else's, is difficult and often leads to frustration. The mind will pick up the suggestion and embed it in the unconscious mind. This is an especially important message since many suicidal people think of suicide as leading to peace, the opposite of frustration. The idea that "all of my troubles will be gone" is undermined by a story that paints a picture of death as difficult to achieve. There is also an air of foolishness and clumsiness about the whole story.

A second suggestion is the description of Rasputin's stubbornness and unwillingness to die easily. The man fought for his life and would not go quietly. So the indirect suggestion is that life is a gift worth fighting for.

The story also connects death with violence. The description of the series of violent acts that eventually caused Rasputin's death, paints a picture that is not pleasant, though a little humorous in a dark way. This again contradicts the rosy view of dying as a safe and peaceful process. This unrealistic view of dying as a pleasant relief is often part of the suicidal individual's distorted point of view.

Using indirect suggestions by telling a story was really the only way to proceed with this particular suicidal patient. He had been brought in by a concerned sister, almost against his will. It was clear during our initial interview that he was certain that he wanted to die and that he believed he would be going to a better place. To try to argue with him under these circumstances struck me as futile.

The other option that was not available was to get him involuntarily committed. The reason for that was that he knew the system well and knew exactly what to say and what not to say to a psychiatrist in the emergency room or a mental health facility in order to avoid being admitted involuntarily.

So the only strategy open to me was to try to reach his unconscious mind, where the deeply entrenched beliefs in the advantages and value of suicide and death were lodged.

Another hurdle that needed to be overcome with this gentleman was that he said he did not believe in hypnosis. He had come to my office, he said, to humor his sister and maybe to satisfy a bit of curiosity.

So, instead of a standard hypnotic induction, I asked him lean back into a reclining chair in my office and humor me by letting me tell him some stories that might make him feel more comfortable. I told him that I knew that he was in constant torment and that he had come to believe that enough was enough. I told him that I had known many people who had come to the same conclusion. I wanted him to know that his conclusions about the advantages of death over life were not unprecedented and that others had been in that dark cold place but had eventually found light and warmth.

I continued with a rambling one-sided conversation until I could see James begin to relax. Then I continued with the indirect induction with a technique that I call "riding the elevator". In this story, I asked James to pretend that he was a little boy again enjoying the pleasure of riding an elevator up and down a skyscraper while all of the adults are busy elsewhere. He is all alone and can enjoy the elevator and the feeling of it stopping and starting as much as he wants. I told him that there are 99 floors and that we will start our ride at the top, where he had already ridden.

I asked him to close his eyes and to begin the ride with me. I then proceeded to describe how he was playing with the elevator control panel. First he rides from the 99th floor down to the 95th floor, and I counted out the floors as they passed by. Then he returns to the 99 floor, this time pressing the button for the 94th floor. Then back up to the 99th floor again and then down to the 89th floor. For a while, I took him for a ride down five more floors with each trip and then back up to the top again. Then I changed the pattern to seven floors down and five floors up, and then up to the 99th floor. I continued to make the patterns of up-and-down increasingly complex and confusing.

Causing confusion and distraction of the conscious mind can be an excellent way of freeing the unconscious mind to bring the conscious mind into hypnosis. Another way of saying this is that distraction occupies the conscious mind so that it stops getting in the way.

When you start doing this work on yourself, you might think about recording some stories or situations that might confuse your conscious mind when you play back the recording, allowing you to bypass your own resistance and take yourself into hypnosis. It's kind of like playing a trick on your own mind in order to achieve the goals that you want to accomplish.

The story of the death of Rasputin, which I told after the indirect induction above, gives you an idea of what an indirect suggestion might look like. I'd like to give you some further examples so that you can create some indirect suggestions for yourself or for loved ones that you wish to help.

To be a successful story for indirect suggestions, the story should not be exactly about what it's really about. If that sounds like double-talk, it is a sample of what indirect suggestions are like. So read the following brief story and see if you can detect the camouflaged messages embedded in the story.

Back in the old days, the source of entertainment in most homes was to listen to the radio. There was an old man who was somewhat hard of hearing. He lived alone and his major source of information and entertainment came from a big old Magnavox radio. The only problem was that he often had a hard time sorting out the static from the voices and the music being broadcast by the radio station. Sometimes, he would be so frustrated that he would give up and go do something else for a while. But he always returned shortly to his radio because he really wanted to hear what was on the station.

Now this old man had a young teenaged boy as a neighbor. And the boy would do yard work and other chores for him. This young boy also was a kind of electronic hobbyist who liked to play around with radios and record players and other electronic equipment.

One day, the old man confided in the boy his frustration with listening to his radio. The boy thought hard about the situation and suddenly came up with an idea. He said to his neighbor, "I'll be back tomorrow and I'll fix you up with something that will change your life."

The next day, the boy returned with a strange-looking contraption attached to some wires. He also had some other odd-looking circuits. He proceeded to disconnect the old man's speaker and install what he called earphones. The old man was very fond of his radio and at first was reluctant to have this kid take it apart. But he got thinking about it and realized that the radio had become almost useless to him the way it was. So he agreed to let the boy work his magic.

After about an hour of work, including some soldering and wire cutting and other seemingly magical procedures, the boy was ready to let his friend try out the new equipment. He showed the old man how to put the earphones on. There were large and clumsy, being an early generation of such equipment, but soon they were firmly placed over the old man's ears. When he turned on the radio, the old man practically jumped for joy, so clear and distinct were the sounds coming directly into his ears. He never again returned to the old way of listening to a radio.

This story is about a radio, two neighbors, a speaker, some wires and soldering and a new set of earphones. But, with a little imagination, you can see that it could be indirectly about using self-hypnosis to improve your reception of the messages coming from your dreams. So telling yourself this story over and over again, even though it may seem to be a strange thing to do, can have a strong indirect affect on your dream recall.

Further, this indirect method of giving post-hypnotic suggestions is useful far beyond learning to better recall your dreams.

This technique was regularly used by one of the greatest hypnotists of the 20th century, or perhaps in the history of hypnosis, a physician by the name of Milton Erickson. He was a master of the art of indirect suggestions and showed over and over again that they can be more effective than direct suggestions because they bypass the listener's natural tendency to resist.

Indirect suggestions have a compelling effect if you know what the message being communicated is all about. For instance, you now know that the story above is not only about old men and neighbors and radios and earphones, but is also about dream recall and the use of hypnosis to clarify and improve reception.

But an interesting thing is that even if you don't consciously know what the message hidden in the story is, it can have a dramatic effect on you. In fact, it seems to be true that when the listener or reader doesn't know what's going on in terms of the communication, the effect is even stronger because it goes straight into the unconscious mind and taps into its power without interference from the conscious mind.

When you're making up your own stories to improve your dream recall or for other purposes, you will always know the double meaning of your stories. Even so, when you record such a story and then repeatedly play it back to yourself, you tend to forget the hidden meaning and the messages go deeply into your unconscious mind.

Now you have an effective technique that you can also use to help loved ones overcome some of the obstacles to their fullest happiness. For instance, if you are a parent, you may already tell bedtime stories to your children. In that context, you can embed some indirect suggestions into stories that you make up.

This possibility could open some exciting avenues of communication with your children. First of all, by creating stories, you are engaging in a very loving and generous act toward your children. Secondly, by employing indirect suggestions, you can help them with their childhood challenges and give them a better chance at success.

For instance, if your child seems to be having an issue with shyness, you could make up a story in which somebody is feeling scared about something. Animal stories are really appropriate for these kinds of indirect suggestions. By using animals, you already remove the story from real life into a fantasy world where the child may not notice the relationship between the animal's issue and his or her own problem, so that the lessons and changes in attitude and behavior seen in the story will begin to show up in the child.

Of course, it goes without saying that if your child has a serious problem of some sort the family physician is the place to start taking action. But if you judge the issues to be normal childhood bumps in the road, these kinds of techniques may prove helpful.

Storytelling and other forms of indirect suggestion have been especially effective with people suffering from post-traumatic stress disorder. Even for those among us who are just troubled by our past, or experience distressing regret, using self hypnosis to reinforce more positive stories and ideas, can be very useful.

My website, www.hypnosisdreams.com, gives you instructions and ideas for using storytelling and self-hypnosis for a variety of self-improvement projects. CDs and downloads are also available there.

This chapter concludes, for now, our discussion of hypnosis and self-hypnosis. We have discussed the use of these tools to tap into the unconscious mind to achieve important life goals. In a later chapter, we will develop more fully a number of ways in which self-hypnosis can be used in the exploration of dreams.

In the next section, we will begin to explore the world of sleep, the world in which we spend nearly a third of our lives. It is interesting how little most people know about this world, which is so full of intriguing mysteries and potential self-awareness and growth.

Chapter 8

Sleep

When I was a child, my uncle used to tell me bedtime stories about his experiences in the army during World War II. One of his favorite themes was about trying to stay awake while on guard duty.

"There I am, the only one awake," he'd say. "Everybody else is asleep because we hadn't rested in almost three days. It's dark and still and I'm bone-tired. My eyes start to close; my ears are ringing. I'm fading fast. I bring myself back with a start and begin pacing faster. I focus every bit of my energy on staying awake. I picture an enemy soldier creeping up just behind a nearby hedgerow. I imagine my own death at his hands should I doze off, even briefly. Then I see a movement over there. I yell, 'Halt!' There's no one there. Someone stirs in a nearby tent and then the relentless silence and stillness returns."

I used to fall asleep before my uncle got much further along in his story. In fact, I now understand that this was his purpose. This was a kind of bedtime hypnotic induction, complete with graphic indirect suggestions for irresistible sleep. And it worked.

His description of the compelling and desperate desire to sleep after prolonged sleep deprivation is accurate. But why is this so? What is the purpose of sleep that we are so driven to drift off? And what consequences would befall us if we found the stamina to resist?

Every night, we all participate in the cycle of life as our turn comes around with the dark side of the earth. As you read this, the people, animals, plants and even single-cell algae are sleeping where it's night, each in their own way.

People have widely differing attitudes about sleep and very different experiences of the process of going to sleep. Here are some examples from elementary school students in a workshop I taught a couple of times.

"It's like marching," said one 9-year-old. "I can hear it and I count my steps as I move along a wide white road, and then I get lost in the fog and forget that I'm marching. When I wake up, I know I've been places but I can't remember where."

Another said, "I hate to go to bed, and when I finally have to, I stay awake as long as I can listening to my radio. That's how I fall asleep."

Still another said, "I have lots of scary dreams. I used to scream for my dad every night, sometimes more than once a night. Now, unless it's really bad, I just tell myself that it's only a dream and I go back to sleep."

These children have described what sleeping is like for them.

Sleep Deprivation

While I was a teenager growing up in the New Jersey suburbs of New York City, my favorite radio disc jockey was Peter Tripp, "the curly-headed kid in the third row," who counted down the top hits every weekday from 5 to 8 p.m. In 1959, as a publicity stunt and to raise money for charity, Peter Tripp set out to try to stay awake for eight days and nights in a Times Square storefront.

I was fascinated. My mother, who was a great believer in the importance of a good night's sleep to maintain health and cure illness, was convinced that poor Peter would either die or go completely mad inside of a few days.

The radio station was really playing up the event with a remote hook-up and periodic check-ins with the night owl throughout their 24-hour broadcast schedule. Nobody had ever stayed awake this long, they said.

After a few days, they announced that a team of sleep research experts had flown in from the University of Chicago's sleep laboratory to study our hero.

With the drama mounting after a few days, Tripp started to sometimes sound a little odd. It seemed my mother might turn out to be right about the risk to his mental health.

I later found out that he began to have serious problems with weak concentration, poor judgment, strong emotions, and feelings of irrational suspicion. These problems were most evident between 2 and 5 a.m. During the day, he was usually OK.

My friends and I were not-so-secretly rooting for something dramatic to happen, like old Peter grabbing an ax and taking after all those people flocking to Times Square to help him stay awake. It looked for a while like the whole thing might end abruptly, either because, as my mother put it, some sane person would realize the danger and put a stop to it, or, because in spite of everyone's best efforts, Peter might just pass out.

But Peter Tripp made it. He finally said "Good night" to all his fans after eight days and nights, plus another eight hours, without sleep. Now we wondered whether he'd sleep for eight days and nights. But, no, he slept for about 13 hours, put in a full day, and then returned to a normal schedule, apparently fully recovered.

Peter Tripp was not the first person or animal to be observed during prolonged sleep deprivation. As long ago as the 1890s, animal studies demonstrated that total sleep deprivation eventually leads to death, usually within three weeks. Studies on humans have, for obvious reasons, not been pushed that far. Eleven days seems to be about the limit.

It seems that the main effect of sleep deprivation in these human studies is the steadily increasing desire to go to sleep. This desire becomes so urgent and compelling that a lot of energy must be spent just staying awake. For the deprived person, even short periods of quiet relaxation inevitably lead to sleep.

Obviously, being a subject in sleep deprivation research requires physical stamina. Young subjects in top physical condition can hang in there. Older or less well-conditioned people will show wear and tear after a few days. It's hard to sort out how much of the decline in concentration, increase in irritability and lack of motivation is the result of the sleep deprivation itself and how much results from the physical exertion required to stay awake.

Soldiers, medical students, emergency workers and others, who are sometimes required to experience sleep deprivation for a few days, can attest to the resulting compelling drive to sleep.

A student in one of my sleep and dreams classes had been a fire ranger in the Pacific Northwest. He told us that after about 60 hours without sleep, he had fallen asleep while operating a chain saw and only awakened when the saw kicked back and just missed severely injuring him.

When asked anonymously, a high percentage of workers on the graveyard shift admit to falling asleep on the job with some regularity. These include firefighters, police officers, train engineers, nuclear power plant workers and even air traffic controllers and airline pilots. In the early spring of 2011, incidents of sleeping air traffic controllers made the headlines. Controllers had fallen asleep on the job in Washington, D.C.; Knoxville, Tennessee; Seattle, Washington; Reno, Nevada; and Miami, Florida.

In a recent survey of airline pilots, more than 50 percent said that they had fallen asleep in the cockpit sometime during the previous year. One pilot admitted that both he and his co-pilot had fallen asleep at the same time for about 10 minutes. Those who are familiar with the perils of the night shift understand that this is just the tip of the slumbering iceberg.

Effects of Partial Sleep Deprivation

Sleep researchers have also studied partial sleep deprivation, which is more common in everyday life. Going to bed too late, getting up earlier than usual, burning the candle at both ends, is almost normal in our modern world. For many of us, getting the sleep we want has to wait for vacations or weekends.

Some people actually report increased energy levels following a moderate decrease in time spent sleeping. In fact, a carefully planned reduction in sleep time has been successful as a treatment for some cases of clinical depression.

So, what price are we paying for sleep abuse? For most of us, more than a few nights of five hours or less of sleep results in fatigue, decreased ability to concentrate, and some degree of emotional irritability and impatience. Surprisingly, however, in one study, eight young adults gradually reduced their nightly sleep time over three months to about five hours. This reduced diet of sleep was then maintained for about six months. While all eight subjects said they were tired much of the time, their performance on a variety of tasks and on measures of mood did not decrease as much as might be expected.

This study and others seem to confirm what many people already suspected from their own experience. Moderate sleep deprivation does not lead to serious health problems.

But what about sleeping or trying to sleep at the "wrong" time? During my college days, I worked in a factory off and on for a few summers. At various times, I worked days, evenings, and the graveyard shift from midnight to 8 a.m.

At first, I liked the idea of the midnight shift, figuring that I would have my summer days and evenings free. But, before long, I was no longer a happy camper.

After a couple of hours unwinding in the morning, I tucked myself into bed with the shades drawn and an electric fan running to try to block out daytime noise. Maybe I'd fall asleep around 10:30 a.m., or maybe I'd toss and turn until noon. Either way, I'd wake up by 4 or 5 p.m. still tired but too restless to sleep anymore.

I'd get up and feel pretty energetic until after the first couple of hours of work. But then it would hit, the passion for the pillow. I felt like Peter Tripp. What a craving I would have around 4 a.m. for just a little nap. As morning rolled around and I knew I would soon be sleeping, I no longer felt as tired. And by the time my new bedtime arrived, I was ready to keep going, only curling up because I knew I should.

What happened to me is regularly experienced by more than 60 million shift workers around the world. Our built-in biological clock is clashing with our work schedule.

Our Biological Clock

The sleep/wake rhythm is wired into our nervous system. Researchers have found a tiny bundle of brain cells near the optic nerve where they are affected by light and darkness. These cells interact with others in complex ways to force their owner to keep regular sleep/wake schedules or pay the consequences. The system is pretty rigid so that when we jet from one time zone to another, we stay on the old time for as long as 10 days. This jet lag happens in spite of the fact that the external world is now providing us a new day/night schedule.

Generations of scientists have found sleep/wake cycles and other biological rhythms everywhere in nature. In the 1700s, biologists noticed that the activity level of single-cell organisms vary around the clock and that plant cell division is also cyclical.

There are rhythms everywhere. Plants and animals of all degrees of complexity participate in a 24-hour symphony. In studying sleep, the daily cycle, called the *circadian rhythm*, is very obvious.

About 50 years ago, researchers isolated volunteers in an underground room free of any hints about time of day or night. Subjects were provided with all the necessities of life and told to keep whatever schedule they wanted. Some remained for a little over a week; others for nearly a month.

What would your pattern be if you had no idea of the time of day and no schedule to keep? It turns out that the natural human cycle is not 24 hours, but about 25 hours. Under normal conditions, we adjust to a 24-hour schedule, but 25 hours is our built-in preference. Maybe that's one of the reasons why most of us tend to sleep longer during vacations and on weekends.

The 25-hour pattern also explains why jet lag is worse traveling from west to east than the other way around. Traveling from New York to Chicago, where it's an hour earlier, gives us a perfect 25-hour day, whereas the return trip shortens the day to 23 hours, leaving us two hours short of our internal clock.

Body temperature is one measure of where a person is in the cycle. Temperature normally bottoms out during the middle of the night and peaks sometime during the day. Other things, such as reaction time, ability to concentrate, mood and, of course, the tendency to fall asleep, follow the same pattern.

There are some individual differences between people in regard to how the daily cycle plays out. People who say they're morning types indeed show a temperature peak earlier in the day than evening people do. There is some evidence that evening people recover from jet lag and adjust to shift work a little more quickly than morning people.

There is an important difference between sleep pattern disruptions resulting from jet lag and those that are faced by people working the night shift. Everyone eventually adjusts to time zone changes, but not necessarily to shift work. In jet lag, important external events like sunlight, mealtimes, and physical activity sooner or later adjust the circadian rhythm.

The timing and intensity of light is of such importance that high-intensity light therapy has been used successfully for jet lag and to treat the winter blues, also known as Seasonal Affective Disorder (S.A.D.). The dark mood that sometimes sets in during the winter seems to be related to a lack of proper light stimulation. Some people are more sensitive to this light deprivation than others.

Our biological rhythm is a complex thing. As I have mentioned, light and dark can influence our pattern. Also, there is a human hormone called melatonin that influences the cycle. Melatonin concentrations are usually lower in the morning and increase toward bedtime. Sunlight seems to decrease the production of melatonin. This might be one of the reasons that light therapy can help in adjusting to jet lag or in Seasonal Affective Disorder. Synthetic melatonin is available as a dietary supplement and has been shown to help some people adjust their biological cycle.

The special problem with shift work is that sunlight, and most of the activities of the rest of the world, occur on the day shift. This makes it nearly impossible to fully adjust to the ongoing mismatch between clock time and internal time.

This constant mismatch shows up in a number of ways. Shift workers suffer more frequently from a variety of health problems. Specifically, they are diagnosed with digestive ailments more than three times as often as day workers, and with anxiety disorders like phobias up to 15 times as often. Many other disorders show a similar pattern. Fortunately, most of these health problems improve fairly quickly after a transfer to the day shift.

So what have we learned about disruptions in sleep? On the one hand, studies of total and partial sleep deprivation fail to uncover any dire consequences. On the other hand, the one consistent consequence of sleep deprivation is the agonizing desire for sleep. Further, a disruption in our natural circadian rhythm is very problematic. In night shift workers, a combination of chronic sleep deprivation combined with a mismatch between biological time and clock time inevitably leads to significant health problems. It can also lead to disaster when night shift workers involuntarily succumb to sleep.

The Nature of Sleep and its Role in Our Lives

Sleep is more than just a passive state. This is a very important point in the understanding of sleep. Our common-sense view is that sleep is a state of passively not paying attention to the outside world. The truth is that the brain renders us *unable* to attend to, or interact with, the outside world and *unable* to think as we usually do.

It's not just that the car is parked and the ignition is turned off. Someone has taken out the spark plugs, removed the tires and covered the windows with blinds. We're not going anywhere. Or, in a different metaphor, at the instant when you fall asleep, your brain has pulled the plug on the TV. It's an involuntary shutdown and, whether we like it or not, this down time takes up about one-third of our lives.

Why has nature programmed sleep into our brains and into those of many of our animal relatives? Put another way, why is it that those of our ancestors who regularly slept survived, while those who didn't, died out? At least five explanations have been offered:

Conservation of resources: This theory relates sleep to hibernation. Animals that hibernate during the winter have the advantage of burning very little energy and therefore needing little or no nourishment during a time when food is scarce. Nightly sleep is a mini-hibernation and conserves energy, helping us get through lean times.

Staying out of trouble: As every parent knows, sleeping is the only time you can be sure your children will stay out of trouble. So too with our ancestors. Saber-toothed tigers were excellent night-time hunters and probably efficiently removed from the gene pool many of our ancestors who were up and out of the cave after dark. There is some evidence that various animal sleep patterns are related to survival needs. For instance, horses sleep briefly now and then around the clock. In the wild, this allows them maximum time for grazing and minimum time in one place, where they might be cornered by predators.

Repair time: Sleep might be for rest and recovery. No kidding. Billions of people go to sleep at night and wake up the next morning more or less ready to face life again. But wait. There are a couple of problems here. First, sudden death through heart attacks occurs most often during the early morning hours rather than late in the evening. If sleep is so restful, why do people with weak hearts die during or right after a good night's sleep? Second, one stage of sleep, called R.E.M. sleep, which occupies about one-quarter of sleep time in adults, is anything but physically restful. (More about that later.) In addition, marathon athletes do not seem to require more sleep than the bedridden.

Reprogramming the memory banks: A good time to commit new information to memory is just before you go to sleep. Researchers have long believed that turning new memories into permanent memories in the brain (a process called memory consolidation) is at its best during sleep. Also, the old advice to "sleep on it" has also had its share of validation. There is evidence that stress gets reduced, and emotional reactions to traumas get smoothed out, during sleep.

The restoration of biochemical balance. Scientists interested in sleep have long been looking for some specific chemical in the body that gradually builds up during waking time, eventually accumulating somewhere in the body until it finally puts us to sleep. Then sleeping reduces this chemical to the point where we wake up.

Years ago, experimenters transfused spinal fluid from sleep-deprived dogs into normal dogs. The normal dogs promptly fell asleep. Some studies have confirmed these results; others have not. A strong piece of evidence against such a simple sleep substance theory is the fact that both human and animal Siamese twins sleep independently in spite of sharing the same circulatory system.

Nevertheless, a number of promising sleep-inducing substances are being investigated. One group, called peptides, originate in the intestines, not the brain, which might explain why a nap often seems so inviting after a big meal.

Speaking of naps, what does the sleep research say about the benefit or harm of napping? And, is it true, as some insist, that getting a little sleep is worse than getting no sleep at all?

In general, studies favor napping over no sleep at all. In one military study, 100 percent of the troops going without sleep during mock war games made fatal mistakes during the first four days. About 48 percent of those getting only 90 minutes of sleep a day survived the week. The survival rate at three hours of sleep a day was 91 percent.

The reason many people believe that a little sleep is worse than none, is probably the phenomenon of sleep inertia, which is the temporary decline in the efficiency of all kinds of mental and physical functioning following sleep. It's as though the nap-taker is still half-asleep for a while. Sleep inertia is especially dramatic when one has not had enough sleep and has to get up and function anyway. Even at its worst, however, sleep inertia only lasts about 15 minutes. Then the benefits of having slept begin to kick in. So the verdict on naps seems to be positive as long as they're not frequent or long enough to interfere with night-time sleep.

In the next chapter, you'll learn what a typical night's sleep looks like. This is sometimes called the architecture of a night's sleep. Each night's sleep is an adventure and is more complex than you might think.

Chapter 9

A Night's Journey

Only since the first sleep laboratories opened in the 1950s have scientists had any idea of what a night's sleep really looks like. Now, six decades later, there are thousands of sleep laboratories and sleep disorder clinics around the world where volunteers and patients sleep while sleepless researchers monitor their every breath, heartbeat and brainwave.

One of the first and most unexpected discoveries of early sleep research was that a night's sleep is made up of a repeating cycle of four stages of one kind of sleep, alternating with a single stage of a second, radically different, kind of sleep.

But before I describe these five stages of sleep I want to tell you about the interesting twilight zone between being awake and being asleep. While we are in this transition, we pass through a state of consciousness called hypnagogic sleep. Because we are headed for unconsciousness, we usually don't remember the vivid images that frequently occur during this state. But if something awakens us at the right time, the images are likely to be recalled in detail.

As mentioned in the chapter on self-hypnosis, this twilight zone is fertile ground for the planting of post-hypnotic suggestions. In addition, the images and ideas that wander through our minds during these times have sometimes turned out to be gold mines of creativity. In a later chapter, we will talk about the special place of hypnagogic dreams in the history of creative and inventive dreaming.

After passing through hypnagogic sleep, we enter Stage One of non-rapid eye movement sleep (non-REM). During this stage, just over the frontier from wakefulness, brain waves, heart rate and breathing slow, muscles begin to relax and eyes are mostly still. A person awakened during this stage, will probably tell you he wasn't asleep at all. The Stage One experience is just down the road from lying back quietly and thinking.

After about 5 to 10 minutes, sleep deepens into Stage Two non-REM. This stage lasts about a half-hour and is marked by a continued slowing of the various biological functions as well as the appearance of brain wave patterns only seen during sleep. Someone awakened at this point will be aware of having been asleep but will usually continue to describe his mental activity as a kind of thinking, imagining or daydreaming.

Stages Three and Four together last about 35 minutes and are so similar that they are referred to collectively as slow wave sleep. Vital signs indicate a body at deep rest.

Very slow brain wave patterns, called delta waves, appear in Stage Three and become more prevalent during Stage Four. Trying to wake someone during slow wave sleep can be challenging and sometimes results in a partly-awake state where the lights are on but nobody's home. Some especially deep sleepers are just about impossible to awaken during stage Four. People usually don't have much, if any, recall from these deep levels of sleep.

The fact that almost all sleepwalking and sleep-talking take place in these deep levels of sleep shows that there is some mental activity going on even though we don't usually remember it. In fact, sleepwalkers and talkers rarely remember the interesting performances that their wide-awake relatives and friends find unforgettable.

So, after about 80 minutes, we have gone through all four stages of non-REM sleep. Non-REM sleep is also called quiet sleep, non-dreaming sleep, or orthodox sleep. The culmination has been the profoundly deep and restful slow-wave sleep of Stage Four.

REM Sleep

At this point, sleep shallows back to Stage Three for a few minutes, then to Stage Two for a few minutes more, and then the first episode of rapid eye movement (REM) sleep gradually but dramatically begins. Lasting only 5 to 10 minutes, this first REM period is just a sample of longer stretches of what some early researchers called paradoxical sleep.

They had a hard time believing the bizarre readings they were getting on their monitoring equipment. During this unexpected stage of sleep, eyes dart around rapidly; the heart might slow and then suddenly speed up. Blood pressure and respiration are also unpredictable. The brain, which was so quiet during slow-wave sleep, now sometimes seems to be even more active than while awake. Wake someone from REM sleep, and he'll almost always recall a dream.

REM sleep is the biological production and projection system of our dreams. Thanks to REM sleep, dreams are not just the remote imaginings of the sleeping mind. REM sleep is the system through which the brain creates a virtual reality for the dreamer.

During REM sleep, the brain is experiencing the dream literally and acting out dream episodes through the same brain circuits as when awake. As part of this process, the motor areas of the brain are acting out all of the events in the dream. If I am slugging it out with someone in a bar room brawl, my brain is sending signals to my arms to punch and to my legs to get with the footwork. Fortunately, there is a mechanism in the brain stem that blocks all of these messages from reaching the arms and legs and other parts of the body. Because of this, we are essentially paralyzed during REM sleep. Otherwise, we'd be running around the room, bouncing off the walls, acting out our dreams.

Similarly, the sensory experiences of a dream are real, not just imaginary. Waking imagination can get pretty vivid but is of a lower level than what happens in dreams. There are measurable physical reasons why this is so. During a dream, the stimulated areas of the brain are the same ones that would be stimulated if the events in the dream were actually happening in the physical world. No wonder dreams seem so real.

What is the purpose of rapid eye movement sleep? Why does our nervous system come equipped with this night time holodeck? This is a question that has puzzled sleep researchers since the early days of the field of sleep study. If sleep is about rest and recovery from the stresses of the day, why should we spend precious downtime in such a strenuous and active stage of sleep?

Since rapid eye movement sleep is the engine of dreams, a psychological explanation involves trying to understand the purpose of dreams. Dreams provide a time of deep self-exploration. While the dreamer is safely tucked away, the sleeping mind can push aside inhibitions, exposing buried thoughts, desires and creative explorations in the form of dreams. Then, upon awakening, the person can return to a sane and ordered life without any harm being done.

This explanation makes sense for adults, but does not account for why newborn infants spend more than three-quarters of their sleep time in REM sleep. We might agree that a newborn does have a great deal of mental processing to do. But the idea that an infant has psychological issues to work through during dream-time, seems a stretch at best.

A biological explanation seems to better address this issue and also fits well with recent research. This accounting of REM sleep is based on the idea that the intense brain activity of REM sleep is a way of opening up new neurological pathways and closing down old, no longer useful, pathways. The newborn is very busy establishing new brain circuitry. As adults, we also are called upon to process each day's events and decide what is worth remembering and what needs to be discarded. REM sleep may be part of the process through which a lot of this occurs.

After a few minutes, the first REM period usually gives way to Stage Two sleep, marking the end of the first full cycle of sleep. Sometimes a sleeper will wake-up briefly between the end of REM and the transition into stage II sleep. Either way, the cycle repeats itself and then repeats itself again throughout the night, each cycle lasting about 90 minutes. The second time through, there will be less deep wave sleep and more REM sleep. By the third cycle, deep wave sleep will last only about 10 minutes, while REM sleep will generate a full 40-minute dream extravaganza. If one sleeps into a fifth cycle, deep wave sleep will probably not occur at all and brief awakenings may interrupt REM sleep. At this point, Stage Two and REM sleep are most prevalent.

Sleeping Babies

Newborn babies have a sleep rhythm quite different from an adult's. For one thing, newborns spend over three-quarters of their sleep time in REM sleep, compared to 20 to 25 percent in adults. The newborn's REM sleep is called active sleep because the total paralysis seen in adults is incomplete in the infant. Arm, leg, face and body movements are common, as are vocalizations. Eyes are sometimes partly open.

In addition, the infant's sleep cycle is not yet established into the day/night cycle. Instead, sleep occurs evenly around the clock, usually in three- to four-hour episodes. A 60 minute cycle through the stages is present instead of the 90-minute adult cycle. Sometimes, instead of going into non-REM sleep first, newborns go directly from wakefulness into REM.

Newborns sleep about 17 or 18 hours a day. As the amount decreases with age, so does the proportion of REM sleep. By three months, sleep time is down to about 16 hours, and REM sleep to about 40 percent of that. By six months, the baby sleeps about 15 hours and spends about a third of that time in REM sleep.

By this age, the overall pattern of sleep has become similar to the adult pattern. There is a day/night cycle and a more adult-like non-REM pattern. The trend toward needing less sleep, and spending less of it in REM sleep, continues at a slower pace right into adolescence.

Two-year-olds sleep 12 hours; 4-year-olds, 10-½ hours; and 10-year-olds, 9-½ hours. The adolescent reaches the adult average of 7-½ hours per night and 20 to 25 percent REM sleep. Of course, all of these sleep times are approximate because there are significant individual differences in the amount of sleep needed.

Children sleep deeply and generally wake up only once, if at all, during the night, (unless, of course they've had a lot to drink.) Almost a quarter of their sleep time is spent in Stages Three and Four, the deepest stages of sleep. Changes in the pattern of sleep continue throughout adulthood. By age 30, the percentage of deep sleep is already down to 15 percent, and there will probably be two or three brief awakenings each night.

As any senior citizen will testify, the sleep of the elderly is fragmented and shallow. On average, 9 or 10 awakenings occur during the night with no more than10 percent of sleep in Stages Three and Four. Slow wave Delta sleep may not be seen at all in the brain waves of some otherwise healthy older sleepers.

Even if we don't wake up during the night, all of us change our sleep position a number of times. My older brother was a notoriously deep sleeper. He would sleep through thunderstorms, family crises, alarm clocks, and sometimes even a dousing with ice water. Yet, by morning, his bed was in total disarray. The sheet was wrapped around his torso two or three times; blankets were on the floor; and pillows between his knees. In hindsight, my brother was apparently prone to vigorous and frequent sleep movements.

All of us move around a lot more during our sleep than we realize. Generally a minimum of two postural shifts take place per sleep cycle, or between eight and 12 per night. A bad night of tossing and turning involves 30 to 40 shifts of position. If we count every little move and twitch, sleep researchers and their cameras record as many as 200 sleep movements during the average night.

There is one particular movement that occurs just as we are entering Stage One sleep. It is a sudden jerk or spasm-like sensation accompanied by a feeling of falling and catching oneself. Most people have experienced this at one time or another. It is called a hypnic jerk. It is probably caused by the brain incorrectly interpreting muscle relaxation as falling. Muscle relaxation is a normal part of dozing off to sleep. But the primitive brain might misinterpret what's going on. Of course, any perceived danger of falling calls for a quick response. The hypnic jerk is the brain's response. It's a kind of reflexive attempt to catch yourself. If you have this experience regularly, you can take comfort in the fact that there is no evidence that it is a sign of any kind of disorder. For many people, it seems to be a normal part of going to sleep.

Even while we are asleep, we are not totally oblivious to our external environment. We respond differently to different kinds of events in the world around us.

Intelligent Night-time Awakenings

In the spring of 1965, my bride and I moved into a modest second-floor apartment in a quiet neighborhood in Rutherford, N.J. We had noted the nearby railroad tracks, but it was not until 2 a.m. on the first morning in residence that their thunderous significance became clear. From a dead sleep, we bolted from the bed in unison as the windows rattled and the furniture shook in accompaniment to the general roar. The noise of two more locomotives barreling through our bedroom that night caused our opinion of our new home to deteriorate. After only a few nights, however, the multi-decibel assault no longer propelled us instantly to our feet. And after a week, I noticed that my wife was sleeping through all but the 6 a.m. express. I soon followed suit and, by the second month, the scraping of wheels, clanging of crossing bells, and the general rumbling of the earth failed to wake us. In a word, we had adapted.

Our baby boy arrived a few months later and we worried that our acquired resistance to night-time noise might render us incapable of responding to the infant's cries of distress. Our worries proved groundless. In spite of our continued ability to sleep through the roar of diesel engines, both of us were awake at the first whimpering from our son.

Over the years, I've heard many other stories of people awakening due to minimal but significant signals. A businessman was awakened by the lack of his clock radio's illumination, telling him the electricity had gone off. This intelligent awakening prevented him from missing a flight to attend an important business meeting. A mother was roused by the nearly silent sound of the cat jumping into the baby's crib. An older man woke up smelling smoke so minimal that upon awakening, he only checked the chimney to make sure, discovering a life-threatening situation. As a child, I used to sometimes wake up my older sister by standing in her bedroom doorway and staring at her. Within a minute or two, she'd open her eyes and look at me. It never failed. I always claimed special mental powers for this. But in truth, I might have cleared my throat or shuffled about a little bit. Still, it was impressive.

All of these examples seem to fly in the face of our usual understanding of sleep as a time when we are totally unconscious and out of touch with the outside world. Sleep research validates these examples, forcing us to re-examine our view of sleep. Studies show, for example, that when researchers use brain wave analysis to spot reactions, sleepers respond to even very faint sounds during all stages of sleep. Further, meaningless sounds are largely ignored, while meaningful sounds, such as a voice saying one's name, result in a much stronger response.

My father never used an alarm clock but was always able to awaken at a time dictated by the upcoming day's schedule. Though I don't trust myself to the point of turning off the clock radio, I find that I almost always awaken just before the set time. I also have made a little game of guessing what time it is before I look at the clock when I awaken in the middle of the night. I am rarely more than 10 or 15 minutes off. Many people report similar experiences. It seems our ability to keep track of the passage of time is not significantly impaired during sleep.

Need for Sleep

We have discussed how sleep deprivation negatively affects us. But how much sleep do we need? And is it the same for everyone?

A few years ago, a couple came to see me hoping that I might help them settle an argument about how much sleep is needed and whether a person's sleep requirements can be changed. The young man began by saying that during his college years he had trained himself to get along on between five and six hours of sleep per night. Now, three years after graduation and six months into his relationship with his very tired-looking companion, he was still thriving on this reduced amount of sleep.

His bleary-eyed girlfriend told me she had always required about nine hours of sleep in order to be at her best. She had a job that required her to get up by 6 a.m. on weekdays. Since moving in with him, she was staying up until 1 a.m. or later most nights and felt tired and miserable most of the time. He was telling her it was all in her mind and that she'd get used to it if she'd just hang in there. "Just think," he would say, "how much more we can be together if we don't waste so much time sleeping."

It turned out that I didn't have to referee a long-term fight over this issue because both of them were anxious to find a way out of the impasse. He could see her suffering and had figured out that what had worked for him was not doing it for her. She was feeling like a wimp and was apologetic. So, all I had to do was give them the old psychologist's wish-wash and say that we really don't know whether or not each person has a biologically set sleep budget. Some researchers say yes. Others say maybe not. I added that the confusion is probably due to the fact that while some people can learn to function well on reduced sleep schedules, others, probably most of us, can't. This explains their contradictory results.

Each of us tends to sleep a certain amount of time each night unless circumstances prevent it. This amount varies from person to person, with about two-thirds of us getting between seven and eight hours per night. Very few people report being rested on less than six hours of sleep, and equally few say they need more than nine hours. Researchers have found a few extremely short sleepers needing three, two, and in the one case of a retired nurse, only one hour of sleep.

Both human and animal studies show the amount of sleep needed is a genetic factor that runs in families. In addition, people living in the Arctic in the months of continuous daylight or continuous darkness will still average seven to eight hours of sleep per night. Astronauts sleeping in space and people living on the streets show the same average sleep requirement.

There are no remarkable differences between short- and long-sleepers in intelligence, personality and life success. As a group, college graduates sleep about as long as unskilled laborers. Thomas Edison was a very short-sleeper. Albert Einstein was not only a long-sleeper but enjoyed sleep and took notice of his dreams. There does seem to be a slight relationship between amount of sleep and longevity. Those who get right around the average of 7-½ hours live the longest, while both the longer and shorter-sleepers die a little earlier.

Getting too much sleep can be as much of a problem as getting too little. Sleeping in on a weekend morning does not necessarily leave us feeling rested and alert. In fact, a sudden increase of two to three hours of sleep increases errors in tasks requiring concentration, increases reaction time, and sometimes can lead to mild or even moderate depression. It also has been shown to produce a small but measurable reduction in problem-solving ability. These negative consequences of getting too much sleep have been called the Rip Van Winkle effect.

What about sleep and exercise? At this very moment, parents around the world are running their children ragged in the hope that the extra physical exertion will make them sleep longer and more deeply. While this assumption makes perfect sense, sleep researchers have had a difficult time confirming it. Studies seem to show that increased exercise leads to a little more deep sleep during the first cycle of the night. After that, however, there are no differences between exercised and non-exercised subjects. Even bedridden individuals require about as much sleep as they used to before becoming bedridden.

Earlier we discussed the rhythm of being awake and being sleep that is part of our daily life. We also discussed the delicate nature of this rhythm and the things that can happen when it is disrupted, as in jet lag or working the night shift.

In the next chapter, we will talk about what is known about individual differences in this rhythm that make some of us happier and more alert in the morning while others of us don't really hit our stride until afternoon or evening.

We will also discuss an extreme example of being a night person. There are some people who are unable to get their biological clock off the night shift. They are stuck with an internal circadian rhythm that is upside down. If this condition is not understood and dealt with properly, it can ruin a person's life.

Chapter 10

Day/Night People

You probably already know whether you are a morning person, a night person or somewhere in between, but look over the following questionnaire to firm up your sense of where you stand in this regard. There is no answer key or scoring system, so just look at the questions and draw your own conclusions.

Early bird or night owl questionnaire

- At what time of the day do you generally feel your best?

- About what time would you get up if you had no morning obligations?

- About what time would you go to bed if you had nothing you had to do the next morning?

- Do you usually wake up on your own or do you use an alarm clock?

- Do you consider yourself to be a "morning person" or an "evening person"?

- How wide awake do you feel during the first hour after you wake up in the morning?

- How hungry do you feel during the first hour after you wake up?

- On an average day, how easy or difficult is it for you to get out of bed in the morning?

- At about what time in the evening do you feel tired and want to go to bed?

- At what time of day would you choose to take an important exam?

- Let's say that you have gone to bed three hours later than usual. If you have no morning obligations, how much later than usual would you get up?

- If someone persuaded you to work out physically between 7 and 8 a.m., how well do you think you would do?

- If someone persuaded you to work out physically between 11 p.m. and midnight, how well do you think you would do?

It might be interesting to share this questionnaire with a few friends or family members to see what differences show up. It could be especially informative to compare your answers with those of your partner.

A preference for one part of the day over another does not seem to be just a matter of habit that can be easily changed. Instead, the preference is more like a built-in daily time clock that varies from person to person. This time clock is biological in nature and seems to run in families.

Gordon the Incurable Night Owl

The following story is an example of an extreme form of this preference. This may very well be one of the most important stories in this book because it will be describing a sleep disorder that affects thousands of people in the United States but is rarely diagnosed. Because it is often not recognized, the sufferer is often accused of being lazy, anti-social or both.

Gordon was brought to my office by his Uncle Harry. Uncle Harry had previously stopped his decades-long habit of chewing tobacco through hypnosis and self-hypnosis. Harry was pretty much the only one in the family who had not given up on Gordon as a lost cause. Gordon was 18 years old and had just been fired from yet another job, this one as a bag boy and cart retriever at a local supermarket. The problem was that, as usual, Gordon was unable to get himself out of bed and off to work with any regularity, even though his hours were from 10 a.m. to 4 p.m. It was still apparently too early in the day for him to get going.

Gordon had quit school at 16, as soon as he was legally able to do so. His father, who was fed up, arranged for him to go live with his uncle because, as the father put it, he was no longer able to stand the sight of his deadbeat son.

Gordon had been given a number of different diagnoses over the years. At age 12, he had been diagnosed with what is called oppositional behavior. That diagnosis is given to children who seem to be hell-bent on not playing by the rules and defying any and all authority figures, including teachers, parents or anyone else in charge. In the professional opinion of the child psychologist, staying awake well past a reasonable bedtime and sleeping late in the morning or into the early afternoon was a form of rebellion. The prescribed treatment involved establishing a program of proper discipline through the systematic use of rewards and punishments. The program was a complete failure in modifying Gordon's behavior.

At age 14, he was taken to the family doctor because he could not go to sleep before about 3 or 4 a.m. Then, of course, he could not get up in the morning. His mother thought that his problem was not rebellion after all, but maybe a medical condition. Sure enough, the family doctor diagnosed him with chronic insomnia and prescribed a sleep medication for him. Gordon managed to go to sleep around midnight but still had a problem getting up for school, so the physician prescribed a stimulant to help him get going in the morning.

This cocktail of medications worked for a few months but had the side-effect of kicking off a severe episode of depression. Gordon secretly stopped taking the medications and reverted to his former sleep pattern of going to sleep around 4 a.m. and dragging himself out of bed usually around noon. Sometimes his mother would literally throw ice water on him to try to get him up in time to go to school by 8 a.m. But waking him up was such an ordeal that she eventually gave up. As a result, Gordon either missed whole days of school or went in for the afternoon.

Gordon had been considered a behavioral problem for years. But now that the depression had become chronic, the school psychologist finally referred him to a psychiatrist. The psychiatrist confirmed the diagnosis of depression and put Gordon on a combination of an antidepressant and a mood stabilizer. The side effects were so horrendous that Gordon attempted suicide by taking all the sleep medication that he had left over from the earlier prescription. He told me that it was not so much that he wanted to die but that he couldn't stand the anxiety, the shakes and the feeling that he was jumping out of his skin. Pharmaceutical companies admitted years later that such side effects not infrequently push depressed teenagers closer to suicide. Gordon believed that he must stay on the medication in order to combat the depression that was supposedly the cause of wanting to stay in bed for half the day. But he couldn't stand the side effects. He felt as though there was no place to turn to relieve his misery.

Because of his chronic absence from school, Gordon was not only failing miserably but had no friends and had become a social outcast. It was no wonder that he took a shot at ending it all.

Gordon's Transformation

Gordon told me this painful story and asked me to put him into the deepest possible hypnosis in order to make him get up in the morning and go to sleep at a reasonable time. My heart went out to this 6-foot-three 220-pound deeply troubled young man. Gordon cried when he told me how grateful he was to his Uncle Harry for not only taking him in but getting him one job after another. He said he knew how terribly he had let his uncle down.

Gordon's visit to my office at that particular time was a stroke of happy coincidence. I had just recently learned of a condition called *delayed sleep phase syndrome*, in which the sufferer is permanently, biologically, set on the night shift. I was amazed when I read about it and even more amazed when Gordon showed up at my door.

To understand the syndrome, let me remind you of our earlier discussion about the circadian rhythm that is biologically built into us. Humans and all animals have a natural biological clock. Most animals are diurnal, meaning that they are biologically set on the day shift. But some are nocturnal, meaning that they are biologically set on the night shift. Like most mammals, humans have a built-in diurnal clock. But somehow there are a few people who, like bats, coyotes and leopards, are set on a predominantly nocturnal daily rhythm. This is what delayed sleep phase syndrome is all about. Such people are wired in such a way as to make conformity to the clock time that is expected of people in our society virtually impossible.

I told Gordon and his uncle that Gordon could go to a sleep disorder clinic, where the diagnosis could be made with certainty. But, since there was no health insurance and no money to pay for such a visit, they decided against such a step.

So, essentially, I told Gordon and Uncle Harry that his problem was not that he was lazy or oppositional or a deadbeat, but that he was simply unable to function on a typical day-shift lifestyle. I told them that since they had come to me requesting hypnosis, I would hypnotize Gordon, not to try to force him into a normal sleep pattern, but instead to try to undo some of the huge amount of negative self-image material that had been piled on top of him for so many years.

Within three sessions, Gordon appeared at my door a changed young man. The haunted look in his eyes was gone and his step was light and cheerful. At my recommendation, Harry had found him a job that fit his nocturnal schedule. He was now driving a taxi on the 4 p.m. to midnight shift. Gordon would then go home, relax for a few hours, watch late night TV, go to bed at around 4 a.m., and almost immediately go to sleep. In addition to his sleep phase disorder, Gordon required a little more sleep than average, functioning at his best with around nine hours of sleep. So Gordon would sleep until about 1 p.m. He would arise feeling refreshed and well-rested and still having a few hours to himself before having to be at work.

The transformation in Gordon's life was dramatic and inspiring to witness. His depression vanished and his insomnia was a thing of the past.

Gordon got back in touch with me a few years later to tell me that he had earned his GED and was now taking evening classes at the local community college to prepare to become a first responder with the fire department. He had been told that they were always looking for qualified people to work the unpopular evening shift. Of course, that would be perfect for him, and he was really looking forward to the future. Meanwhile, he had reconciled with his father and, for the first time in his life, had a steady girlfriend.

I hope that this story might make a light bulb go on for some readers who know somebody like Gordon. Of course, not all people who have trouble keeping to a daily schedule are suffering from this disorder. Clinical depression can indeed interfere with a reasonable daily schedule. Other psychiatric diagnoses, including drug and alcohol abuse, may be involved. But if all of these causes are ruled out, there may be reason to pursue the possibility of a sleep phase disorder.

We have been discussing various kinds of disruptions in the usual daily rhythm of sleep and wakefulness. Gordon's condition of delayed sleep phase syndrome is one kind of sleep disorder. There are many others. It is to those other disorders that we now turn our attention.

Chapter 11

The Sleepwalker Killing

The 1997 movie *The Sleepwalker Killing* was based on a true incident. In the early morning hours of May 23, 1987, in Toronto, Canada, a 23-year-old man named Kenneth Parks got out of bed, walked to his car and drove over 15 miles to his wife's parents' house. There, he fatally stabbed his mother-in-law and seriously wounded his father-in-law. He then drove to a police station and turned himself in, saying that he thought that he might have killed somebody.

The prosecution appeared to have an open-and-shut case. The physical evidence was overwhelming and the defendant had confessed to the crime, though he said that he didn't remember doing it. The only thing missing was a motive. Kenneth Parks and his in-laws had always gotten along well, and there was no evidence of any recent quarreling or tension in their relationship. Further, he had nothing monetarily to gain, and there had been no evidence of robbery.

Except for fleeting images, the defendant claimed he had no memory of the crime. Neither did he have any memory of the drive to his in-laws' house nor the trip to the police station.

His legal team mounted a defense based on the assertion that he was not responsible for his actions because he was sleepwalking at the time of the crime. The jury agreed with the defense and on May 25, 1988 returned a verdict of not guilty. Kenneth Parks walked out of the courtroom a free man.

How is it believable that a person could engage in such complex behaviors over an extended period of time and still be asleep and therefore not responsible? A related issue is that while the usual waking mind is asleep, there must be some other level of the mind that is awake, because the behaviors are clearly intentional in some sort of way. What was the sleeping mind thinking it was accomplishing? Where in the mind did the violence come from? These are challenging questions.

The defense attorneys in the Kenneth Parks case reconstructed a story of what happened that the jury found believable. They pieced together that, first of all, Kenneth Parks had a history of sleepwalking. An expert witness testified that in persons with such a history, sleep deprivation and stress can lead to dramatic episodes of sleepwalking. Kenneth Parks had been experiencing both. He was unemployed and had accumulated significant gambling debts. He had apparently slept little or not at all for several nights preceding the night of the attacks.

In a state of sleep deprivation, such a person may enter a deep sleep-deprived stage of sleep. At the same time, the stress may lead to a heightened state of vigilance which can result in the partial awakening that is the mental condition necessary for sleepwalking to occur. There is a kind of tug-of-war between the forces that are keeping the person in a state of deep sleep and the forces that are stimulating the person into a state of arousal. In this in-between state, the sleeper's actions are directed by very primitive mental functioning. In this condition, basic emotions like fear and rage can cause the person to leap into action because of the lack of the usual restraints and inhibitions that the wide-awake mind contains.

In the Kenneth Parks case, the defense described a series of events that seem to have been the immediate triggers for his murderous assault. They argued that he had been interrupted by one of his in-laws that night while trying to accomplish a repair of a heat duct in their house that he had earlier in the day promised to fix. When he arrived at their home, he was asleep. He had a key and let himself in and was apparently beginning to focus on the needed repair when he was interrupted. Somehow, his primitive sleeping mind interpreted the interruption as a life-threatening assault on him. He did not recognize who he was attacking.

It has been determined that sleepwalkers are unable to recognize faces. Parks viciously lashed out in retaliation at a person he thought was a stranger, perhaps an intruder, and a threat. But where did the knife come from? The defense made the case that one or the other of the victims had retrieved the knife from the kitchen in an attempt to help the other who was being assaulted. In fact, Kenneth had defensive knife wounds on his hands from apparently grabbing the knife from the wrong end as he was wrestling it away from one of them, probably his mother-in-law. From his point of view, the defense argued, the whole sequence of events unfolded as a series of misunderstandings on the part of his sleeping, but partly awake, mind. To his sleeping mind, these misunderstandings led him to believe that he, or perhaps the very people he was attacking, was in danger. His still-sleeping mind did the only thing that it knew how to do. It counterattacked.

This was not the first time that a person who committed a murder was acquitted with a sleepwalking defense. In 1981, in Scottsdale, Arizona, Stephen Steinberg killed his wife by stabbing her 26 times. He was acquitted in 1982 because the jury was convinced that he had no idea what he was doing at the time of the murder because he was sound asleep. There is not a lot of detail available concerning this case, so I will move on to a third case in which the defendant was convicted in spite of a sleepwalking defense. The third case contains many interesting twists and turns and has been widely studied.

Again, as in the Kenneth Parks case, there was no doubt that Scott Falatar committed a murder on the night of January 16, 1997. His victim was his wife, Yarmila. And, as in the Kenneth Parks case, Scott Falatar claimed to have no memory of what he had done or why. He and his wife Yarmila were Mormons and active in their church. Scott was an elder. They had two teenage children. Scott had a degree in electrical engineering and had a responsible position in a successful company. The couple rarely disagreed and had never been known to seriously quarrel. There had been no arguments on the night of the crime, and there was no substantial insurance money to be gained. So again, as in the Kenneth Parks case, there was no apparent motive for the murder.

The Falatar case, however, had a couple of complications that the Parks case did not. These complications led to there being significant hurdles for the sleepwalking defense to overcome. The biggest hurdle was that not only had Scott stabbed his wife repeatedly, but he then walked into the garage, changed his bloody clothing, put on gloves, returned to the area on the pool deck where he had stabbed her, and proceeded to roll her dying body into the water in an apparent attempt to finish her off by drowning her. He was successful. We know all of this because a neighbor, Greg Koons, had heard Yarmila's screams and was in a position to look over the fence into the yard. He had not seen the initial attack and at first thought the person lying on the ground had simply fainted or passed out. When he saw Scott begin to drag Yarmila toward the pool, he thought it might be an attempt to revive her. He was horrified to realize that Scott's intentions were deadly, and it was at that point that he called the police.

By the time the police arrived, Scott was back in bed apparently sound asleep. He reported that he was roused by the sounds of sirens and the commotion downstairs as the police entered the house and began to climb the stairs. According to his statements, these were his first memories since going to bed and quickly to sleep about an hour and a half earlier. He further reported that he was confused and dazed and wondering why the police were there. Was there an intruder? Were his wife and children safe? And why had they handcuffed him?

Just as in the Kenneth Parks case, the prosecution thought it had a slam-dunk. The evidence was clear and included an eyewitness to at least part of the attack.

The defense attorneys argued that almost all of the elements necessary to make a diagnosis of sleepwalking disorder were present in this case.

The diagnosis of sleepwalking disorder is accepted by the American Psychiatric Association. The following are some of the conditions that must be met in order for this disorder to account for violent criminal behavior.

First, the incident must occur within the first hour or so of sleep. That is when the person is in the deepest levels of sleep. Scott Falatar had fallen asleep at about 9:30, and it was at 10:30 that his neighbor witnessed him rolling his wife's body into the pool. So the entire attack had occurred during the first hour of sleep.

Second, the sleepwalker must have no memory of the event in question. Scott Falatar was adamant that he remembered nothing between the time he fell asleep at 9:30 and when he heard the police at about 10:45. In fact, he asserts to this day that he still remembers none of it.

Third, there must be no attempt to cover up the attack. Here is where the Falatar case gets a little bit complicated. Scott did change out of his blood-soaked clothing and went upstairs and washed up. But he did not clean the blood from the knife that he used to stab Yarmila. Neither did he do anything to hide or dispose of the bloody clothing or remove blood from his neck and part of his face. Also, he made no attempt to dispose of the body. So the defense argued that the murder was carried out in a manner that was guaranteed to clearly demonstrate his guilt. Was Scott Falatar really that stupid, they asked? The lack of an effective cover-up does seem to meet this third requirement.

A fourth requirement for a diagnosis of violent sleepwalking is that the perpetrator is insensitive, even oblivious, to his surroundings. Yarmila's screams were loud enough to be heard by a neighbor but apparently had no effect on Scott.

Another important consideration is to rule out other explanations for the attack. The usual suspects are things like extreme anger during a fight, financial gain, jealousy, or other understandable motives. Other possibilities are drug or alcohol abuse or a psychiatric condition. All of these had been ruled out.

Another important element is the state of mind of the perpetrator after the fact. This, of course, is a judgment call. But the diagnosis describes a person who is full of shock and remorse and baffled by what has taken place. In both the Kenneth Parks case and the Scott Falatar case, the confusion, shock, remorse appeared to be authentic.

Also important is whether or not the person has a history of sleepwalking. Scott Falatar did have such a history. The evidence is even stronger if there is a pattern of sleepwalking in the family of origin. In the Falatar case, the court ordered a family tree to be constructed which demonstrated that there were many members of the family who were sleepwalkers, bed-wetters, and who suffered from night terrors, all of which are deep sleep disorders.

And finally, there must be no rational reason for the crime's commission. The crime must make no sense. In both of these cases, there is no motive, nothing to be gained, and a great deal to lose.

The outcome of the Scott Falatar trial was the opposite of the Kenneth Parks trial. Falatar was convicted of first-degree murder and sentenced to life in prison without the possibility of parole. The jury did not buy the sleepwalking defense. Apparently, the major issue for them was the fact that some time after the stabbings, Scott returned to his wife lying next to the pool and rolled her into the water. The jury did not believe that this second homicidal act could have been the behavior of a sleepwalker.

We have already mentioned that sleep deprivation and life stress can trigger episodes of complex sleepwalking. Another contributing factor that has made the news is the use of the sleep medication Ambien. One news report describes a woman who took an Ambien, went to bed, and about an hour later got up without getting dressed. She then got in her car and drove to a busy downtown intersection where she got into an accident. She reportedly then urinated in the middle of the street, punched out a police officer and had to be restrained. She later had no recall of any of these actions. There have been other incidents in which Ambien or similar sleep medications have been implicated.

There is another sleep disorder that on the surface seems similar to violent sleepwalking behavior but is really quite different. It is called rapid eye movement behavior disorder (RBD). Sleepers with this disorder act out their dreams. You may recall that during rapid eye movement sleep the parts of the brain that would normally fire up when we engage in the actions of our dreams actually do fire up.

That's why dreams seem so real. Your brain is literally experiencing the dream, and the actions in the dream take place with full brain involvement. So unless there were a mechanism to prevent it, we would all be running around the room, bouncing off the walls, engaging in whatever activity we're dreaming about. This doesn't usually happen because most of us are essentially paralyzed. Somewhere in the lower part of the brain there is a mechanism that keeps us from acting out our dreams.

In those suffering from RBD, this mechanism breaks down. So instead of lying in bed dreaming that they are trying to fight off a robber, sufferers get up out of bed and go through the motions that are called for in the dream. Needless to say, this disorder can cause significant damage to furniture and other objects and bodily injury to the dreamer and to those who happen to get in the way.

While getting up during the night and behaving in sometimes aggressive ways are common to both of these disorders, they are really quite different. Sleepwalking disorder occurs during the deepest levels of non-REM sleep, whereas RBD occurs during REM sleep. Sleepwalkers rarely remember anything of what they did during sleepwalking. RBD victims, on the other hand, usually have pretty clear recall of what they did and what exactly the dream they were acting out was about.

RBD occurs almost exclusively in older men, with an average onset of age 60. It is often associated with other neurological problems, such as Parkinson's disease, stroke, or brain injury. Sleepwalking has no such association with neurological problems and, if anything, occurs more often in younger men and women.

Sleepwalking almost always happens in the first few hours of sleep, when sleep is at its deepest while RBD happens toward morning when a higher percentage of sleep time is being spent in REM sleep.

There are medications that can be effective in treating RBD. Still, it is recommended that sufferers take precautions to protect themselves and others, such as placing the mattress on the floor, removing dangerous or breakable objects from the bedroom, and sleeping alone. In some cases, it is recommended that the person sleep in restraints.

In the next chapter, I will recount an amusing but less dramatic example of sleepwalking behavior. Then we will talk about other sleep events and sleep disorders, including sleep apnea, narcolepsy and insomnia, the most common sleep disorder of all.

Chapter 12

Sleep Disorders

Let's talk some more about sleepwalking. Sleepwalking is best thought of as a partial awakening. Contrary to popular opinion, it is not the result of acting out a dream since it does not occur during rapid eye movement sleep. Instead, it occurs during the deepest levels of sleep, sometimes referred to as slow wave or Delta sleep.

Sleepwalking is fairly common among children and seems to peak in its frequency among 9 to 12-year-olds. It decreases after that, but one survey found that about 5 percent of college students called themselves regular sleepwalkers and about 15 percent of adults report that they've sleepwalked at some point in their lives.

We will be discussing other sleep disorders later in this chapter. But before moving on, I want to share an interesting episode of sleepwalking. This one is from my private practice.

Twice during the past week, Charlene had found clear evidence that sometime during the night someone had urinated into the clothes hamper. She was pretty annoyed the first time and confronted her live-in boyfriend Drew, who denied any wrongdoing. Charlene remained convinced that he had done it in drunken protest against her increasingly shrill complaint about him leaving the toilet seat up in the middle of the night. They'd been having quite a few fights lately, and she had come to expect most anything from Drew after he'd had three or four beers, which was about how many he'd had on the night in question.

They'd gone round and round about the incident. Drew finally conceded that perhaps he had gotten up and done it without having any recall of the event. He said he certainly did not intend such an unworthy form of protest.

Then, about a week later, the phantom struck again and Charlene was fit to be tied. Drew later said that describing her as breathing fire would be an understatement. The only clothes in the hamper were Charlene's, since Drew generally let his clothes collect in a pile on the closet floor. Drew further inflamed the situation by saying that the urine in question smelled an awful lot like Charlene's. That did it. "How can you say that?" Charlene said. "That is so stupid. What do you mean it smells like mine? What does mine smell like? And how would you know? You're pathetic."

Drew knew he'd been acting kind of like a jerk lately. On this second eventful night, he might have had a little too much to drink and had slept a deep dreamless night's sleep. Maybe he was getting weird. But the hamper did smell like the bathroom smelled after Charlene had been in there. And hadn't she and her sister told stories of Charlene's sleepwalking adventures during their youth?

It was Charlene who came up with a plan, elegant in its simplicity. They would set a video to capture an ongoing picture of the bedroom closet for the entire night. Each morning, they could erase the recording if the phantom urinater had not appeared. The first six nights, the hamper remained dry. Charlene had been taking the clothing out of the hamper and sticking them under the bed before she went to sleep. After six nights, however, she decided that maybe it was safe and left the clothes where they belonged. That did it. The phantom struck again.

Charlene could hardly wait for Drew to be exposed. There had been a party at their place the night before, and a few people had crashed on couches and floor space in the living room and guestroom in order not to have to drive home. Charlene invited them to witness Drew's anticipated humiliation.

Fast forwarding through the video captured mostly a deserted closet door and hamper. Then there was a shot of Drew staggering past on his way to the bathroom to leave the toilet seat up yet again. And then it happened. Charlene's image appeared on the edge of the field and lingered there for a moment. Then while standing, she removed her pajama bottoms, walked over to the hamper, straddled it, and with a steady stream soaked its contents.

A week later, Charlene was in my office telling me her story and asking me if she was certifiable.

Sleepwalking runs in families and is related to being a deep sleeper. One of my clients, a regular sleepwalker, reported waking up in the middle of the night during a family reunion weekend and finding one of her siblings and two of her cousins wandering around the house. At the morning breakfast table, another cousin told her that she herself had later joined the promenade. It is also common for sleepwalkers to be sleep talkers, and many of them also were bed-wetters during childhood. Adults who continue to sleepwalk usually do so only occasionally.

Observers of sleepwalkers often refer to them as looking like zombies or spooky ghost-like characters. This is probably because of the slow and deliberate way in which sleepwalkers tend to move. The ghostlike impression is probably amplified by the sleepwalker clearly being oblivious to the people around her, who may be talking and otherwise trying to get her attention. It does seem that the sleepwalker is in her own world.

Waking the sleepwalker is difficult and sometimes nearly impossible. There is usually no danger in attempting to do so, although in rare cases as seen in the last chapter, the results can be disastrous. Short of the murderous examples in the previous chapter, there are some sleepwalkers who do emerge from deep sleep displaying aggressive behaviors, but they usually persist for only a minute or so while the person is in the process of awakening.

Narcolepsy
Sleepwalking is only one of dozens of different kinds of sleep problems. Sleep disorders are divided into two broad categories.

The *dyssomnias* are things like not being able to go or stay asleep (insomnia), or sleeping too much *(hypersomnia)*, uncontrollable daytime falling asleep (narcolepsy), or having difficulty breathing during sleep (apnea).

The *parasomnias* are things like sleepwalking, nightmares, night terrors, bedwetting, (enuresis) sleep paralysis, and rapid eye movement behavior disorder (RBD).

At age 36, the Rev. Charles Nelson was beginning to wonder if he was starting to feel the effects of getting older. He was aware that he had always needed more sleep than most people. He had earned a reputation during his high school years for falling asleep on the school bus fairly regularly and, on several occasions, being awakened by the bus driver at the end of the line, way past his stop.

But what had been happening to the Rev. Nelson lately was different. He was not just falling asleep during boring TV shows or monotonous bus rides or on lazy plane trips.

One day, he sat in his office following a 20-minute nap and recounted recent episodes. He had fallen asleep twice during denominational district meetings, once during a telephone conversation with a friend, once during a marriage counseling session with two of his parishioners (who thought he had been drinking), and, most distressing, twice while driving his car. Both car episodes resulted in his driving off the road, but luckily neither resulted in any injury or significant damage.

The Rev. Nelson displayed all of the classic symptoms of *narcolepsy*. He found himself being unable to stay awake during the day, even after having had adequate sleep the night before. He found that taking a nap when drowsy helped some, but even that didn't guarantee his staying awake if things got quiet.

Then he began to experience another kind of sleep attack. Instead of falling asleep gradually, he found himself suddenly losing all muscle control. On more than one occasion he collapsed to the floor. During these attacks, called cataplexy, he would remain somewhat conscious of his surroundings but be unable to move. He described these episodes as being half-awake and half-asleep. The physical paralysis was frightening. So was the fact that such episodes usually took place during a time when something emotionally intense was going on, not in response to a boring environment. The first time such an attack occurred, he was home alone watching a DVD of the movie *Schindler's List* and found himself getting upset. Then, suddenly, he was lying down on the sofa where he had capsized and was unable to move.

It seems that attacks of cataplexy are essentially periods of rapid eye movement sleep intruding into waking consciousness. This experience of sleep paralysis is related to the paralysis that normally occurs during rapid eye movement sleep.

Finding the cause or causes of narcolepsy has been a challenge. In recent years, however, researchers at Stanford University's Center for Narcolepsy have been making progress in uncovering its roots. It seems that there is a strong but complicated genetic predisposition for the disorder. Having the genetic tendency, however, is not enough to bring on narcolepsy. There must also be an environmental trigger. The triggers might be things like a viral infection, a trauma, or intense life stress.

It is probably correct to say that *rapid eye movement behavior disorder* (RBD) and *sleep paralysis* are two sides of the same coin. In both cases, the mechanism that keeps us from crashing into walls while acting out our dreams is not functioning properly. In the case of sleep paralysis, the mechanism continues into wakefulness. In the case of RBD, the mechanism is too weak and breaks down while the dreamer is still asleep.

It is not uncommon for otherwise normal sleepers to experience a little taste of one or both of these disorders. In the informal surveys I have done of my psychology students and dream group members, about 10 percent report having experienced at least occasional episodes of being unable to move upon awakening. These experiences might be called brief episodes of cataplexy. A smaller percentage report that this can last for several minutes and is downright scary. Another 10 percent or so have occasionally had the experience of acting out the last few seconds of a dream as they are waking up. These episodes are small samples of RBD and usually involve little more than sitting up in bed and maybe throwing one last punch at an imaginary opponent.

The Rip Van Winkle Disease

There is sleep disorder that might be a dark and sinister second cousin of narcolepsy. The story of Rip van Winkle and the fairytale of Sleeping Beauty may very well be rooted in historical fact. A devastating disease has come to light in the last 15 years or so in which victims sleep away weeks, months or even years of their lives.

Called Kleine-Levin Syndrome (KLS) with the technical name *Recurrent Periodic Hypersomnia,* the disease most often strikes teenagers. The average age of onset is about 16 years. It is a rare disease with about 500 victims worldwide.

However, it is as destructive as it is rare. The first episode occurs suddenly sometimes after a flu-like illness. The victim goes to bed as usual but instead of waking up the next morning, continues to sleep and sleep and sleep. During short breaks in sleep, the victim eats and goes to the bathroom. During these brief periods of semi-wakefulness there is bizarre, childlike and impulsive behavior.

This pattern goes on until suddenly the victim wakes up and returns to being completely normal until the next episode. Typically upon awakening, there is no memory of the previous weeks or months. It's as though a whole chunk of time has been taken out of their life.

The average duration of each episode is about 12 days. But sometimes the person may sleep for several months at a time. The episodes can continue to reoccur over a period of 10, 15 years or even 20 years or more. The mother of one sufferer in her twenties calculated that her daughter had slept for over four years of the previous 12 years. Victims of the disease miss out on graduations, family events and years of schooling.

Because the disease is so rare and the symptoms so bizarre, very few physicians have any idea what is going on with their young patients.

So, many families go through the added torment of dealing with health professionals who accuse their teenagers of faking their symptoms or just being lazy and manipulative. Many such families have been reported to child protective agencies for alleged abuse or neglect. In some cases families have gone from doctor to doctor, and only after searching for a year or more, finally find a professional who has the expertise to make a proper diagnosis.

A diagnosis can be comforting because at least the family has a name for the suffering. But unfortunately, there is no known cure for the disease. It just has to run its course. For about 90% of patients the episodes do eventually stop.

The causes of the disorder are unknown. But there is a strong indication that there is a genetic component, as is the case in narcolepsy, that predisposes a person to develop the disease following an environmental trigger.

When Insomnia Kills

In the last couple of chapters, we have been discussing a variety of sleep disorders that provide us with dramatic examples of things that can go wrong in the sleeping and waking cycle of our days and nights.

We now turn our attention to insomnia, the most common sleep disorder. For most of us, insomnia is usually a troublesome but not debilitating experience.

There is one form of insomnia, however, that always kills its victims. *Fatal Familial Insomnia* is a disease that, as the name indicates, runs in families and always ends badly. It is a genetic disorder that is present in only about 40 families worldwide. All of these families can trace their lineage back to a man who died of the disorder in Venice, Italy in the year 1765.

The victim of Fatal Familial Insomnia leads a healthy life until the disease strikes, usually around the age of 50. The patient's inability to sleep is dramatic from the beginning and gets worse as the weeks go by. Within a month, the person is not sleeping at all.

By the second month, the sleeplessness is taking its toll on the emotional life of the victim. Anxiety, irrational fears and increasing suspiciousness and paranoia dramatically interfere with daily life.

What started off as a troublesome inability to go to sleep escalates into a seriously frightening long-term insomnia. The victim and the family become increasingly panicked that the insomnia will not go away. This is usually the time during the progression when medical attention is sought.

By about the fourth or fifth month, the relentless wakefulness begins to lead to a deterioration of all of the usual mental functions that we take for granted. Concentration, short-term memory and verbal abilities become increasingly compromised.

Although sleep is unattainable, consciousness begins to resemble a kind of twilight zone where hallucinations and dreamlike experiences begin to be mixed together with waking reality. The Hollywood movies *The Fight Club* (1999) and *The Machinist* (2004) both vividly depict protagonists living in this kind of dark and confused world.

Within a few more months, a rapid and progressive weight loss occurs. Other physical symptoms include high blood pressure, elevated pulse rate and profuse perspiration.

The disease then progresses to a point where virtually all bodily functions are chaotic and out of rhythm. Meanwhile, the mental state of the sufferer has deteriorated to irreversible dementia, which is indistinguishable from other dementias like late stage Alzheimer's disease. Death usually occurs in about a year, but with considerable variation.

This disease was unknown until quite recently. It turns out that Fatal Familial Insomnia is one of a class of diseases referred to as prion pathologies. A prion is a malformed protein. In the brain, it causes cells to become misshapen and lose their ability to function properly.

Fatal Familial Insomnia is caused by a prion that is the result of a genetic mutation. Most prion diseases, however, are the result of infectious transmission. Mad cow disease is the most well-known example.

Since a deterioration of the structure and function of the brain progresses as the disease advances, it has been difficult for researchers to determine exactly what causes the death of a victim of Fatal Familial Insomnia. Is it the destruction in brain tissue? Or is death the result of the total sleeplessness itself? It is probably the case that, while the rapidly accelerating brain damage would eventually kill its victims, the process is greatly speeded up by the insomnia. The immediate cause of death is usually the insomnia.

Common Forms of Insomnia
Fatal Familial Insomnia is a dramatic but rare form of the disorder. Let's now turn our attention to the more common experience that most of us have struggled with from time to time.

What are the consequences to health and well-being that result from the milder types of insomnia? Many of the same difficulties mentioned in an earlier chapter as resulting from sleep deprivation also apply to insomnia. Daytime fatigue, decreased efficiency and difficulty concentrating are among the first casualties. Sleep-deprived people also report feeling irritable, anxious and sometimes depressed. These outcomes should be taken seriously because taken together they can affect interpersonal relationships, job performance and physical safety.

What do we know about the causes of insomnia?

In the 2002 Hollywood film *Insomnia*, Al Pacino stars as Detective Will Dormer, who fatally shoots his partner during a confused attempt to pursue a fleeing suspect. The shooting seems to have been an accident. The situation however, is more complicated than that. The partner had just told Detective Dormer that he would testify to internal affairs regarding earlier misconduct by Dormer.

The movie has a twisting psychological plot. It culminates in Detective Dormer's death but not before we witness his psychological torment from relentless insomnia.

The film dramatically depicts a commonly assumed connection between insomnia and a guilty conscience. It is not unusual to hear an outraged person ask a dishonest perpetrator how in the world he sleeps at night.

Although a guilty conscience may indeed lead to sleepless nights, the multitude of possible causes of insomnia makes the situation considerably more complex than that.

If, in a survey, people are asked if they are currently having problems with sleep, almost a third of them will say yes. If we take that result at face value, insomnia is a huge epidemic. The situation gets foggier when more questions are asked. For instance, maybe it's not exactly insomnia when the sleeplessness is being caused by something else. When that is the case, it is called secondary insomnia.

What are some of these other causes of sleeplessness? A psychiatric diagnosis of clinical depression or anxiety disorder often leads to difficulty sleeping. Physical pain from injuries or conditions such as arthritis might be the culprit. Further causes might be the use of drugs or alcohol or trying to sleep at irregular hours.

If the insomnia seems to have none of these causes but has occurred out of the blue and has lasted for more than a month, it is called primary insomnia. In the survey mentioned above, about one in five people having trouble with sleep are suffering from primary insomnia. This puts the primary insomnia rate at about 6 percent of the population.

So what do you do if you are having trouble sleeping? The first answer is to look over the issues mentioned above to see if they might be leading to sleeplessness. Things like drinking too much coffee or alcohol, being in pain from a sprained ankle, being depressed, being anxious and worried are some of the real-life everyday causes of insomnia. Addressing these causes of sleeplessness is the first step in dealing with insomnia. The following case describes one interesting cause of insomnia.

Brad had been troubled by waking up frequently during the night. Sometimes he was able to go back to sleep and sometimes not. Either way, he was pretty wiped out the next day. And this was happening more and more regularly. None of the usual suspects that can cause insomnia were present.

The mystery was solved after he moved in with his girlfriend Tammy. The very first night, she found herself awakened repeatedly by Brad thrashing his legs around in bed. She said it was like sleeping with a soccer player who is still acting out the game in bed. After two or three nights, she had several bruises on her legs and ankles from being kicked.

It turned out that Brad was suffering from restless leg syndrome. Brad had long known that he often had a difficult time sitting still during the day and also while trying to go to sleep at night. During boring meetings at work, he sometimes had to make a huge effort to stop himself from jiggling his legs. The urge to do so was sometimes overwhelming. He described the sensations as having an itch that can't be scratched. You can't get at it, but moving your legs relieves some of the discomfort. Still, he hadn't made the connection between that and his frequent awakenings during the night. Tammy immediately saw the connection.

As you might expect, restless leg syndrome is caused by some kind of disruption in the usual functioning of the nervous system. Interestingly, almost 20 percent of cases can be cured with dietary iron supplements to treat iron deficiency anemia. Apparently, the iron system is closely related to the functioning of a neurotransmitter in the brain called dopamine. The lack of iron causes a disruption of this system. Restless leg syndrome is the result. After checking Brad's iron levels, his physician prescribed an iron supplement which dramatically decreased Brad's symptoms within a few weeks.

A cautionary note: It is dangerous to self-medicate with iron supplements since high levels of iron can be toxic, especially among older people

There are more than a dozen other possible causes of restless leg syndrome. Among them are low blood sugar, diabetes, fibromyalgia and thyroid disease. In addition, a variety of medications can bring it on or at least make it worse. Antidepressants, antipsychotics and antihistamines have all sometimes been the culprits.

Are there any general rules of thumb or tips that might help all of us sleep better?

The United States National Library of Medicine has published some tips for overcoming insomnia. Some of these are worth mentioning. They include: drink warm milk at bedtime, practice relaxation techniques like meditation or self-hypnosis, avoid alcohol, caffeine or tobacco, get some physical exercise early in the day, avoid naps, reserve your bed only for sleeping or sex, and keep a regular sleep schedule. If you still can't sleep, get up and try again later, and keep your bedroom as dark as possible – maybe even get rid of illuminated clocks.

The performance of a choral composition comprised of some sleep tips was premiered in New York City by Cantori New York on November 1, 2008. It is a 6-1/2 minute voice and woodwind performance. The choral piece was composed by the acclaimed concert pianist and composer Beata Moon, and it was performed in all seriousness and is a lovely musical piece. It also would be great music to go to sleep by with all of its indirect suggestions for sleep.

The above information and tips for getting a better night's sleep are contained on my website, www.hypnosisdreams.com. A script for using self hypnosis to improve sleep is also on the website. Also available on the website is a recording I prepared of the script. Many people have found this professionally prepared recording to be most effective.

We have discussed how sleep deprivation has significant effects upon daytime performance. But what of the long-term effects of insomnia on health and longevity? As mentioned earlier, sleep deprivation has few if any long-term effects. And a recent survey even suggests that mild insomnia can actually lead to a longer life.

As mentioned in the earlier chapter, more severe sleep deprivation, especially when sleeping at the wrong time as in shift work, does leave people vulnerable to a wide range of physical and psychiatric illnesses.

A survey of over 1 million people conducted by the American Cancer Society found that most sufferers of insomnia actually have a lower mortality rate than non-sufferers. In fact, sleeping more than 8-1/2 hours a night is related to a 15 percent increase in mortality rates compared to sleeping between 6-1/2 and 7-1/2 hours a night.

Only when the insomnia is so severe that sleep is reduced to less than four hours a night does the risk to mortality increase. So this means that getting one extra hour of sleep a night above the norm of 7-1/2 hours is worse for your chances of living a long life than getting two or three hours below the norm. That outcome is rather surprising.

These statistics should be comforting to insomniacs, who often feel that their insomnia is something that might seriously affect their health. While it is clear that night-time sleeplessness does lead to a whole bunch of negative daytime consequences, impending death is not one of them.

It is apparent from our discussion of sleep disorders that sleep is a fragile state in which a variety of things can go wrong. Still, it is a compelling state of consciousness which pulls all of us into its grip every night.

This chapter on sleep disorders wraps up the section of this book covering sleep.

In the following chapters, we will turn our attention to the dreams that bubble to the surface of our sleeping consciousness.

Chapter 13

Dreams and the Unconscious Mind

So here's the question: Who makes up our dreams? When I go to sleep at night, I don't make a decision about what my dreams are going to be. I go to sleep and sometime during the night dreams are created for me.

I don't say, "I think I'll dream about Aunt Jennifer tonight. I'll have her walking down the street wearing a raincoat and opening an umbrella even though it's not raining. Then she'll try to cross the street but get hit by a taxi. She'll be uninjured but the contents of her purse will spill all over the street and other cars will drive over them, destroying her possessions. And by the way, Jennifer looks an awful lot like my friend Heather. In fact, now that I think about it, I'm not sure which one this dream character is. Then, all of a sudden, Jennifer/Heather starts attacking my father and I really don't know where he came from. Now the street turns into a pasture where golf balls are scattered all over the place and also flying through the air so that I have to dodge them."

This particular dream was one reported by a student of mine a few years ago. We spent a fair amount of time trying to sort out what the dream was all about, and we'll talk more about ways of trying to do that later. But, for now, I'm mentioning the dream as an example of how dreams come from some kind of alien author who doesn't use the same kind of logic that we use while we are awake.

This question of where dreams come from has baffled humans for thousands of years. In the next chapter, we'll get into the various explanations that have been offered over the centuries. But I want to start out by taking a shortcut to the end of the story first.

The end of the story involves the widely accepted modern notion of our mind being divided into two parts, namely the conscious mind and the unconscious mind. As we have discussed in an earlier chapter, the term unconscious describes a deeper part of us than just the surface thoughts that we have during our waking life.

The bearded, cigar-smoking genius who developed the idea of the unconscious mind was the famous psychoanalyst Sigmund Freud. It has become popular in the field of psychology to put down this gentleman who lived and wrote about 100 years ago. He has been accused of being rather a dirty old man who found sex everywhere, and a chauvinist whose theories discounted the psychological realities of women even though most of his patients were women. There is truth to these criticisms, but the essential idea of there being a deep part of the mind that we're not usually aware of, has stood the test of time.

Dr. Freud came to the conclusion that there must be a deep reservoir of the mind called the unconscious mind because of two fascinating aspects of human psychological experience. One of them, as already mentioned, is the experience of dreams. Freud, as a modern scientist, rejected the notion still popular at that time that dreams come from some spiritual realm. His view was that a dream-creating mechanism in the unconscious mind does the work. Further, when Freud began to take dreams seriously, he discovered that they were what he called the "royal road to the unconscious." In other words, if you want to know what the deepest part of your mind is all about, you need to learn to understand your dreams.

In order to understand why that's important, we need to recognize that Freud's work with dreams was part of his therapeutic technique called psychoanalysis. And what he discovered was that even though the patient herself might have no idea why a particular set of mental symptoms is troubling her, her dreams always have the answers. So if a patient suffering from, say, a terrible phobia such as a severe fear of going out of the house, analyzing her dreams would lead to an understanding of what was deep inside her that was causing such fear.

The key was to find a way to sort through what seem like bizarre characters and events in the dream and figure out what the unconscious mind is trying to tell us. For not only do dreams come from the unconscious, but the unconscious mind is also the source of symptoms such as anxiety, depression and serious mental illness. So Freud's clinical curiosity about dreams and their source was one of the things that led him to develop his notion of the unconscious mind.

Okay, so it makes sense that it's probably a good idea for mentally ill patients to gain access to the unconscious mind with the help of a mental health professional. But why, you might ask, would you consider doing the same thing?

The first answer is that even in those of us who are mentally healthy, the unconscious mind contains troublesome material that leaks into the conscious mind in the form of unpleasant emotions, poor decisions or annoying forgetfulness. Gaining access to this material can improve the quality of life.

Traditional psychoanalysis was designed and practiced in order to open a line of communication between unconscious and conscious minds. Few psychotherapists practice psychoanalysis any longer. But most therapists have been influenced by Freud's ideas and utilize what is sometimes called psychodynamic psychotherapy. This form of therapy values the art of probing the unconscious mind to work toward increased self-awareness.

Those among us who are mentally healthy and don't wish to seek the services of a psychotherapist, can still profit from this kind of increased self-awareness. It might be helpful, for instance, if I understand that unconscious issues are at least partly responsible for my intense emotional dislike of my boss.

In addition, the unconscious mind contains a storehouse of creativity and insight that is not normally available to our conscious mind. Gaining access to this material can be exciting. This newfound access can lead to creative insights beyond what we thought we were capable of.

When we discuss dream work, you'll read about a lot of examples of your genius within making itself known through dreams.

Many creative people confess that they don't really understand where some of their most brilliant insights and ideas come from. Albert Einstein was a great believer in the wisdom of dreams. Maybe one of the differences between very creative people and the rest of us is that the creative genius is somehow more in touch with his unconscious mind. So, with some practice working with dreams and learning self-hypnosis, who knows what creative adventures await you?

Even for those of us who don't aspire to be Albert Einsteins, there is a lot of inner wisdom available in the unconscious mind for the asking. In working with dream groups, I have often observed people being startled by the insights of their inner minds.

Another reason to learn about dreams is that the whole process can be a lot of fun. Most of us already know that dreams are colorful and full of mystery. But once you learn how to remember more of your dreams and get used to their language, the results can be truly enjoyable. And if you are in a relationship with somebody who might be interested in doing the same thing, the process gets doubly fascinating as you share dreams and explore this hidden realm together. By the way, sometimes people who are really close, such as identical twins, can experience something called dream sharing, where both people have similar dreams on the same night. That can be an exciting thing to have happen and a lot can be learned from it.

Dreams sometimes cleverly tell us to not take dreams or ourselves too seriously. As you begin to remember more of your dreams, you will see a playful attitude bubbling up from your unconscious mind.

I think those of us who work in the mental health field may incorrectly emphasize the negative things that we sometimes find out about ourselves during therapy and other self-improvement work.

I have been struck by the reaction I sometimes get when, at a party or in some other social context, it's discovered that I am a psychology professor. Frankly, the reaction is often pretty negative. One woman actually turned around and walked away as soon as she had that information. Another asked me a question often repeated, and that is: "Are you going to try to analyze me?"

At the bottom of these suspicions is the not unfounded observation that psychologists and other mental health professionals seem sometimes to be looking for the dark side of a person's personality. It is as though the nice, generous, sensible, happy, and moral person that we think we are is just a mask covering the real and nasty underbelly of our personality. Maybe people suspect that hanging around psychotherapists will sooner or later be a downer. They expect to be brought down by having their inner rottenness shoved in faces. What a shame this is. Working with people to help them understand their dreams has repeatedly shown me the opposite of this little scenario.

At heart, we are more playful, more spontaneous, more creative, and usually more generous than we think we are. So please, don't be expecting to find out the worst about yourself. That is not what's going to happen. You may not find out that you are wonderful in every way, but you will discover that there is wonder inside you and miracles to discover there.

In later chapters, you'll learn a variety of ways of working with and interpreting dreams based on what we now, in the 21st-century, know and understand about dreams. Existing side by side with these modern techniques are remnants of earlier ways of thinking about and listening to dreams. So, in the next chapter, I will present an historical overview of how dreams have been understood and worked with over the centuries.

Chapter 14

Dreams, Ancient Understandings

Many animals display rapid eye movement sleep (REM). Since the REM sleep state pretty thoroughly occupies the attention of the sleeper, it's not surprising that animals of prey, such as sheep and horses, spend very little time there. They need to remain alert. Predatory animals, such as lions and bears, sleep up to 16 hours a day and a good chunk of that is spent in REM sleep.

Dogs and cats have sleep patterns similar to our own. Since we can't ask directly, it's an open question whether their REM sleep produces dreams, although most pet owners believe that it does. If so, how do they understand the experience of dreaming? We might wonder if they can tell the difference between dreams and waking reality.

There is evidence that our ancient human ancestors did not make a clear-cut distinction between dreaming and waking life. But as human civilizations advanced, so did people's notions of how to understand dreams. The following story told by my uncle, a long-time missionary to Africa in the 1920s and 30s, displays an interesting understanding of the relationship between dreams and waking reality in a preliterate society.

"Early one morning, as the sun was rising, there was a great flurry of activity and the raising of many voices in the village where we were trying to establish a mission. It turned out that one of the men in the village had challenged another man to a one-on-one fight to the death.

"In order for such a battle to take place, the combatants were required to seek the permission of the Council of Elders and there had to be a good reason. Such fights were not to be undertaken for trivial reasons. Of course, all of us missionaries were very much opposed to such barbaric events and tried our best to prevent them.

"In this case the elders were assembling with some urgency because the particular reason for this battle being necessary was pressing and of high priority, according to the combatants. Since I had become rather liked and accepted by the tribe, I was allowed to attend the Council's deliberations as long as I agreed to remain silent.

"The warrior who was initiating the request for a battle described in detail how he had been brutally assaulted and murdered by his new enemy. There was much discussion about the nature of the murder and details of the attack, the weapon used and so on. The elders wanted to know if there were any witnesses to this treachery. I found myself scratching my head listening to the detailed description of the murder of a man who was sitting before me at that very moment. It just didn't make sense until finally it became clear that the protagonist was talking about a dream that he had had that very morning. And, from the nature of the discussions, it was considered not only acceptable but absolutely required that he avenge his own death through combat with his assassin.

"I was shocked and dumbfounded and attempted to break my silence to prevent such a primitive and barbaric battle based on superstition. But I was rebuked. The battle was to be joined at high noon.

"At the appointed hour, the entire tribe assembled to witness the spectacle, which was to take place in a kind of primitive arena with benches arranged around the circle that surrounded a cleared area. I knew of this arena just outside the village, but I had never seen it used before."

"Much drumming and chanting began about 9 a.m. and slowly mounted to a crescendo at about noon, followed by silence.

"The combatants then appeared in full warrior regalia. Each was carrying a spear but also had a small dagger strapped to his thigh with rawhide.

"The fight was finally joined, with the two combatants clashing spears and repeatedly lunging at one another amid much raising of dust and dirt and yells of encouragement from their kin. Finally, one of the warriors managed to throw the other to the ground and disarm him. But as the victor drew back his spear to aim it at the loser's throat, an elder let out a bloodcurdling scream and the warrior froze in place. The battle was over and the vanquished dream assassin was to be forgiven."

My uncle used to enjoy dragging this story out with all kinds of colorful details, many of which were elaborated to demonstrate the primitive and godless clan system of tribesmen, whom he always referred to as lost souls in need of redemption and the saving grace of Jesus. So, some of the story might be exaggerated. But other sources seem to confirm that the essential elements could well be true.

It turns out that this battle was a little bit like a modern wrestling match in which the combatants were not intending to kill, or even seriously injure, each other but were putting on a kind of mock performance. Another similarity with wrestling was that the outcome was determined before the start of the match. The whole purpose was for the person who dreamed he was murdered to be able to gain satisfaction by this mock murder of his killer.

This story displays an interesting relationship between dreams and dreamers in this preliterate society. It seems apparent that the events that my uncle witnessed were remnants of an earlier time, when dreams were taken as absolutely literal and the revenge was therefore actually carried out with a battle to the death. By the 1930s, when my uncle witnessed this spectacle, the battle had become symbolic. So, by then dreams were not taken literally, but neither was their content completely separated from daytime reality.

A somewhat later idea is that dreams are messages from the spirit world. About 4000 years ago, the ancient Egyptians left many documents about how to interpret dreams as communications from the gods. There are also lots of accounts in the Hebrew scriptures concerning dreams and their interpretations. And around 200 B.C., there were hundreds of sleep temples scattered around Greece where a person could perform certain rites and sacrifices and then sleep in the temple. The resulting dreams were then assumed to be messages from the gods and provided valuable information about all kinds of things, such as financial matters, legal decisions and affairs of the heart.

Viewing dreams as important messages from God is a common theme in the establishment of many religions. In modern times, Joseph Smith, the founder of the Mormon Church, dreamed that an angel directed him to golden tablets that described the American Indians as descendents of the tribes of Israel and recounted Christ's visit to the New World.

In the next chapter, we will begin to turn our attention to modern psychological ways of working with dreams. We will further discuss the revolutionary contributions of two giants in the field of dream interpretation, Sigmund Freud and Carl Jung.

Chapter 15

Freud and Jung

As mentioned earlier, the modern idea that dreams come from a deep place within the dreamer's mind originated with the Viennese physician, Sigmund Freud. He was not the first person to ever use the term unconscious mind, but he was the first to give it a central place in the understanding of the human personality.

To understand Freud's thinking, it is important to know that his view of human nature and the human mind is not flattering. He came to believe that, at its deepest level, the human mind is pretty depraved and packed with animal aggressive and sexual drives. Since we are generally unaware of that, he viewed us as self-deluded or at least un-self-aware. But, during sleep, the truth comes out through our dreams. Many dreams are indeed aggressive or sexual. But according to Freud, even those that aren't, display those themes once properly interpreted.

Freud also revealed to us that there is a lot of baggage in the unconscious mind that was planted there early in our lives. Early childhood experiences and misconceptions live on beneath the surface of our grown-up minds.

Freud said that a dream is a kind of safety valve that allows us to be primitive, childish and crazy during our sleep so that we can return to the relative quiet sanity of our waking minds without being overwhelmed by these urges. A correctly interpreted dream brings us closer to understanding the unconscious mind. That is why Freud called dreams the royal road to the unconscious.

Almost all contemporary dream interpreters have shed Freud's emphasis upon primitive urges as the secret to understanding dreams. But they have retained his view that dreams come from a deep place within the dreamer.

The unconscious mind is not always in a state of peace and harmony in relation to the conscious mind. For instance, a selfish urge in the unconscious mind may push toward the surface and trouble the conscious desire and intention to be generous.

There also are different elements in the unconscious that tend to be in conflict with each other. For instance, a childish desire for revenge may be in conflict with an equally childish longing for approval. Under these circumstances disturbing feelings and thoughts come to the surface and trouble the conscious mind. This is how symptoms such as anxiety, irrational fears, and depression are formed. This is why dream interpretation still plays an important role in what are called depth or psychodynamic forms of psychotherapy.

But even when not in need of therapy, dream work is an excellent tool for improving the quality of psychological and emotional life.

According to some writers, most notably Carl Jung, dream work can accomplish much more than just make us a little more peaceful within ourselves.

Carl Jung, who was Freud's student, later parted company with him in part because of a difference of opinion about how to look at dreams. Jung believed that, far from uncovering only our depths of depravity and inner turmoil, dreams reveal intelligence and creativity that suggest that they come from a source of higher wisdom as well as lower instinct.

Jung is probably best known for his concept called the *collective unconscious*. Jung agreed with Freud that there is material in the unconscious that comes from instinctual urges, early childhood experiences and material that our conscious mind judges as unacceptable. Jung called this part of the unconscious the *personal unconscious*. But in addition, there is a realm of the unconscious that contains memories and themes that have their roots in the experiences of our common ancestors.

Jung observed that religious beliefs, as well as fairytales and dreams from very different parts of the world and different periods of history, have a lot in common. Jung believed that this is because they all spring from the archetypes of the collective unconscious. These inspired creations reflect the wisdom of the ages. They bubble up from the deepest parts of our souls.

In chapter 5, we discussed the archetypes of the collective unconscious in some detail. We said that just as our bodies contain memories from our ancestors in the form of DNA information, so our minds contain memories from our collective past in the form of the archetypes. An archetype is neither good nor bad in and of itself. The archetypes of hero, lover, father, goddess or priest, to name just a few, can bring forth meaning and beauty in life. Under other circumstances, any one of them can lead us into irrationality and destructive behavior. At their best, the archetypes prove themselves to be storehouses of inner creativity and boundless energy. When they are acted out negatively, they can lead to catastrophe, as when the German people confused Adolf Hitler with the hero archetype.

With this view of dreams, it's no wonder that Jung considered them as almost sacred texts. Dreams are like visitations from a world of wisdom, you might say from the world of the gods. Dreams come to us, trying to help us see more clearly and more wisely. The conscious mind is small and limited in its view of itself and the world. But the collective unconscious is far more knowledgeable and has a much more intelligent and informed view. So if we listen to our dreams and learn how to understand their language, we will become more enlightened. Our little conscious mind will become larger and richer through contact with the collective unconscious.

Jung used the term *ego* to refer to the very limited conscious mind that most of us think is in charge. The term ego originated with Freud. Jung demoted the ego from the center of personality, as Freud envisioned it, to a limited un-self-aware entity. Jung used the term *self* to describe the larger personality, which includes both conscious and unconscious material. To Jung's way of thinking, working with dreams will enlarge the ego to include more of the self. In this way, we become more fully what we were meant to be.

Jung believed that the unconscious mind creates dreams to help us become more whole. All of us are incomplete and one-sided in one way or another. If I grow up trying to be a good boy all the time, there is a bad, mischievous boy buried inside of me. If my sister prides herself on being pretty and feminine, there may be a tomboy hiding within her.

In a dream workshop I conducted with 9- and 10-year-old children, a beautiful little girl reported the following dream fragment.

"I woke up screaming because I knew I had done a terrible thing. In this dream, I was not a little girl but a vicious big black dog. I couldn't keep myself from chasing my Aunt Jennifer. She was screaming and running and trying to get away, but I chased her down and grabbed her by the leg and I felt my teeth sink in and it was all bloody. That's when I woke up."

This dream had clearly bothered this little girl so much that she was willing to take the risk of sharing it in front of her classmates. I could sense her shame about it. And I felt the only thing to do was to reassure her that it absolutely did not mean that she was bad or vicious.

As the children were filing out of the classroom, it was obvious that she was lingering as long as possible. So I went over to her and asked her what kind of dog bites? She answered that an angry dog bites. I said that maybe a dog that is frightened bites to keep scary people away. I asked her if maybe she gets scared sometimes, especially at bedtime. She said yes with much feeling. So I said that maybe the dog was there to protect her. Her face brightened and she left the room looking a lot lighter.

This story is meant to illustrate Jung's important insight that I mentioned before. His idea is that dreams balance out what we are like while we're awake. He called this function of dreams their *compensatory function*. That term describes this little girl being vicious like a dog to compensate for her sweet, gentle, and somewhat frightened daytime personality. So the dream is trying to balance out a certain one-sidedness. This girl's dream is saying that she is much more than just sugar and spice and everything nice.

So why are dreams so hard to understand? Why do they seem so baffling and confusing and to make no sense? If their message is so important, why not just say it outright and be done with it?

Sigmund Freud believed that dreams are intentionally disguised by the unconscious mind in order that we not get freaked out by the primitive and unacceptable stuff that's being expressed. The dream expresses it so that it doesn't build up pressure in the unconscious mind and make us go crazy, but it disguises it so we won't get overwhelmed and go screaming into the sunset. Occasionally, the disguise is not good enough and we are freaked out anyway. This is how he explains nightmares. What we're seeing is the underbelly of our unconscious mind, and we don't like what we see.

Carl Jung sees the baffling nature of dreams quite differently. He says that dreams are hard to understand because the language of the unconscious mind is different than the language we speak while we're awake. The unconscious mind speaks a language more like poetry than prose. It speaks in metaphor and figurative speech. It expresses itself in vivid pictures and intense feelings that defy logical description. This different language is not about trying to deceive us. In fact, the unconscious mind is trying its best to get through to us, but we are too thick to understand because we're so used to our conscious kind of language. So learning to understand dreams involves becoming familiar with this other way of thinking and expressing.

During a particularly turbulent period of my life, I had a repetitious dream in which I would be out somewhere trying to use a public pay phone to call home. In every dream, there was some mechanical problem that prevented me from getting through. Each dream was a little different, but the common thread was always one of profound frustration.

It doesn't take a rocket scientist to come up with the idea that maybe the dream was telling me about a problem of communication in my life and that the problem was on my end of the line in spite of the fact that I was busy blaming someone else. Sometimes, the language of dreams is not so obvious, but this dream gives us a hint of how to look at dreams.

In this chapter, we have begun to describe fruitful ways of working with dreams. The writings of Sigmund Freud and Carl Jung have provided an essential foundation for modern ways of understanding our dreams.

In the next chapter, we will present detailed examples and instructions for working with dreams in a number of different ways. This process is not simple. Some people are tempted to buy one of the available dream dictionaries that provide ready-made interpretations of dreams that everybody can apply to their dreams. Such dictionaries are a gross oversimplification of the real nature of dreams, which can only be interpreted individually. I think you'll find the examples in the next chapter to be interesting and enlightening as you proceed to a sense of how you can do your own dream work.

Chapter 16

Dream Work

Keeping a Dream Journal

In order to do meaningful dream work, you'll need to keep a dream journal. The following tips will help you get started.

1. Buy or create a dream journal that is pleasing to you and easy to use. The journal should be of a size to fit on the shelf or table by your bed so you can conveniently write in it.
2. Have a light source available, bright enough so you can see what you are writing but not so bright as to wake you up fully or disturb anyone sleeping in the room with you.
3. Before lying down, put the date at the top of the page and write a sentence or two about what went on in your life that day. This provides a context for later understanding the dreams you remember.
4. When you wake up remembering a dream, write it down as though it is happening right then. In other words, use the present tense. This tends to increase dream recall and helps bring the dream to life.
5. Give each dream a title. A title helps you remember the dream later. Coming up with a title can also trigger an understanding of the dream.
6. Leave a space after each dream so you can later write down ideas of what the dream might be about.
7. Set aside about 15 minutes once or twice a week to look over your dreams and jot down your reactions.

Improving Dream Recall

It's impossible to work with and learn from dreams unless you remember them. If you already regularly remember your dreams, the following tips will increase your recall even more.

1. Before getting into bed, have your journal, pen and light all set up and ready to go. This tells your unconscious mind that you're ready to remember.

2. Before going to sleep, tell your dream mind that you are interested in what it has to say.

3. Spend a little extra time sleeping when you get a chance. Sleeping even a half-hour more than usual increases your time in REM sleep. If you have trouble remembering dreams, this alone may do the trick.

4. If you're still having trouble remembering dreams, drink some extra water before going to bed. That will probably wake you up at least once during the night. The more often you wake up, the more likely you are to recall dreams.

5. Try to wake up slowly. Don't use an alarm clock unless absolutely necessary. Waking up abruptly tends to erase dream memories.

6. If you have the feeling that you can almost remember a dream, but not quite, lie back in the position you were in before you woke up. This can trigger a memory.

7. Re-read your journal from time to time and also try to talk to other people about your dreams. Maybe find a dream partner for mutual dream sharing. These are ways of telling your unconscious mind that dreams are important to you. Your unconscious mind will respond by showing you more dreams.

Also, the bedtime self-hypnosis technique in chapter 6 can be applied to improve dream recall. An effective phrase to use is: "I welcome and remember my dreams."

A recording of an effective script for improving dream recall is available on my website, www.hypnosisdreams.com.

Categories of Dreams

Dreams that Reveal Your World

As you begin to work with a dream, ask yourself if the dream could be telling you something about the world around you. Dreams can sometimes bring you startlingly accurate and insightful information.

If you dream that your best friend has been in a traffic accident, check out the possibility that your dream is in some sense warning about or even predicting such an event. Maybe your friend needs someone to tell him to slow down, get off the cell phone and pay attention to his driving.

If you dream that you end up throwing up after eating some leftover egg salad, maybe you should check out its freshness before you have a food-poisoned lunch the next day.

In my experience in dream classes and workshops, the overwhelming majority of people have had at least one such predictive dream. Many people have had these experiences repeatedly, and most people find the experience somewhat unsettling. People often wonder if such dreams reveal some hidden psychic powers. Later we'll discuss the possibility of what is called extrasensory perception (ESP) showing up in dreams. But for now, I'd like to give you a more down-to-earth explanation that explains many of these kinds of dreams.

Let's take the example of Janice in the preamble. Recall that her dream alerted her and her husband to a faulty latch on a door leading to the patio and swimming pool. If she had not had this warning dream, the door latch might have remained in its broken condition long enough to create a serious danger to their toddler. The dream dramatically depicted such a disaster and really got Janice's attention.

How can the sleeping mind know something so important while the waking mind is apparently clueless?

The most probable explanation is that during the day Janice had noticed something amiss about the door latch, but, being busy and distracted, had not really registered the information in her conscious mind. Nevertheless, on some level she had remembered the observation. And then, while she was dreaming, her sleeping mind put the information into a dream of what could happen if it was ignored. This explanation may not be as dramatic as a psychic powers explanation, but in a way, it is even more impressive. It demonstrates the alertness and intelligence of the inner mind. It also highlights the importance of checking dreams for waking life information that might be valuable or, in this case, life-saving.

A not-so-happy ending was reported by Frank, a physician, following the death by barbiturate overdose of his younger brother Steve, who lived several thousand miles away. Frank had earlier dreamed that his brother had died in exactly the manner he soon did. Frank had pushed the dream out of his mind as irrational, considering that his brother was beginning to get some breaks in his budding acting career. And, as far as Frank knew, Steve had stopped taking mind-altering drugs, legal or illegal.

But, in looking back on the situation, Frank became convinced that there had been warning signs. For one thing, his brother had mentioned some recent sleepless nights. Frank knew that Steve had a history of insomnia and would sometimes over-medicate himself. Not remembering that he had previously taken barbiturates, he would take more. Also, while in the most recent phone conversation Steve had seemed upbeat, he did mention that there were some problems in his relationship with his partner. Frank knew that earlier relationship troubles had led to a suicide attempt.

Frank knew that Steve was very good at hiding his emotions, but that he had a long history of seasonal depression and it was the middle of the winter where he lived in Oregon, a geographical area not noted for its sunshine.

Frank's sleeping mind had put all this together and showed him a possible outcome. Perhaps even if he had taken this warning seriously, Frank could not have prevented the outcome. But Frank was nonetheless disturbed by his lack of action in the face of a danger that he now believed he could have predicted, based on the dream that spelled it out for him.

Janice's dream turned out to be a warning dream. And Frank's dream turned out to be predictive, or what is called precognitive. In this case, we might say that the difference between a warning dream and precognitive dream is whether or not the dreamer pays attention and is able take action.

So, again, these dreams and many others that people have, suggest that it's a good idea to check out the daytime waking world to see if the dream is telling you something that you need to pay attention to.

We've discussed the psychoanalyst Carl Jung before. He was very psychologically sensitive and aware. He reports that, in the year prior to the outbreak of World War I, he had many very disturbing, violent and bloody dreams. At the time, he was working on himself psychologically and repeatedly attempted to discern the inner psychological conflicts and memories that were creating such dreams. But it was only after war broke out that he realized the source of these terrifying images. He believed that we pick up information from the larger world around us and weave this information into our dreams. As you're listening to your dreams, I would suggest that you consider this source of information.

You may find yourself sometimes one step ahead of the news, not because you have extraordinary psychic abilities, but because your sleeping mind sometimes puts together information that you otherwise might ignore. One example was Martha, a teacher who had repetitive dreams about a student bringing a gun to school and opening fire on other students. It was a few months later that the most notorious such event took place in Columbine, Colorado.

In trying to piece this all together, she remembered reading an article in a magazine about the phenomenon of bullying in school and the profoundly destructive effect it has on its victims. The article included descriptions of some attempts by bullied students to strike back. She was also aware of this pattern in her own school and had become concerned about it.

All of the dreams above yielded accurate information when looked at as dreams that reveal your world. These dreams show two different sources of outer world information that can communicated. In the dreams of Janice and Frank, the information came from their personal lives. In the dreams of Carl Jung and Martha, it came from the larger world around them. So being aware of both of these sources can be important.

Dreams That Predict Illness

A number of years ago, I had a dream in which I was being asked by a Red Cross volunteer to donate blood. In the dream I responded that I couldn't donate blood because I had once had hepatitis. In the dream, this seemed to be the correct response. Upon awakening I was left scratching my head because I had never had hepatitis. About a month later, I began to develop symptoms that led to a diagnosis of hepatitis which laid me low for several months.

Was the dream just a coincidence? Or had my unconscious mind picked up some kind of body sensations indicating the early stages of the disease? If so, what kind of sensations could they have been? And how could my unconscious mind have interpreted those vague, hardly perceptible sensations and arrived at the correct diagnosis?

I don't know the answers to those questions, but I have since learned that my experience was not an isolated incident.

In her book *The Committee of Sleep*, Deidre Barrett recounts a number of similar instances of dreams dramatically pointing to an early diagnosis of impending illness. She then goes on to report on extensive study in Russia in which over 1600 dreams of 247 patients were collected and analyzed for possible correlations with medical conditions. The researcher, Vasilii Kasatkin, became so impressed with the sleeping mind's ability to make early diagnosis that he argued that dream reports ought to be an essential part of all medical diagnosis protocols.

In the Russian study, the early detection of cancer was a common achievement of the dreaming mind. Many such dreams specifically pinpoint the location on the body where the malignancy is growing. For instance, one patient who was later diagnosed with stomach cancer, dreamed that a pack of dogs was attacking that specific area of his body.

A growing cancer tumor eventually intrudes into surrounding tissue and organs and the person then feels something. It might be a burning sensation or a feeling of being swollen. Eventually, pain is felt. These consciously perceived sensations are what usually lead the patient to seek medical attention. It makes sense that the unconscious mind might notice some of these before they are powerful enough to be noticed by the conscious mind.

Scientific Breakthrough Dreams

An example of how dreams that reveal your world can lead to dramatic breakthroughs in science and technology is the case of the invention of a workable sewing machine in 1845 by a young machinist named Elias Howe.

Elias Howe was trying to solve the problem of the bottleneck in the production of clothing and other textiles that was caused by the fact that all sewing had to be done by hand. The cotton gin had accelerated the separation of cotton from seeds by a factor of several hundred. Recently invented spinning and weaving machines made those processes efficient as well. Sewing was the only process that continued to require time-consuming hand labor.

One evening, Howe was struggling to come up with a working prototype of the sewing machine based on some ideas that had occurred to him. But as he proceeded, he became increasingly frustrated. Fatigue caught up with him and he dozed off to sleep and had the following nightmare.

He was in the jungles of Africa, where one of his cousins was a missionary and had told him stories about the natives. In his dream, Howe was being chased by a hostile group of cannibals. He fled for a while but was soon caught, bound hand and foot and carried off on a pole to the native village where a large cooking pot had been prepared for him.

When he discovered that his hands were tied loosely he became hopeful of escape from the unpleasant prospect of being served for dinner. With his hands free he tried to climb out of the pot only to be forced by many wooden spears back into the increasingly hot water. The spears clattering against the side of the pot and poking at him became the most vivid images in the dream.

It was at this point in the dream that he awakened in a sweat and almost immediately recognized that the dream had provided an idea for his invention. While dreaming, he had noticed a curious characteristic of all of the spears. They each had a kind of knothole close to the pointed end.

The solution was now obvious. Prior to this dream he had been attempting to design a sewing machine that would pull a thread through the fabric to be sewn in much the same manner as in hand sewing. He had assumed that the thread should be attached as usual to the blunt end of the needle and then pulled through the fabric.

The dream provided him with an entirely novel solution to the problem. The hole in the needle should be in the front, pointed end. The thread should be attached there and pushed through the fabric rather than pulled.

Elias Howe created a prototype using this new design. The resulting machine was a complete success.

Two questions come to mind in regard to this story. The first is: Why did the solution to the problem appear in such an elaborate and bizarre dream context? The second is: How did the dreaming mind know the answer to a problem that had the waking mind stumped?

The answer to the second question is that the waking mind in some sense knew the answer to the riddle but was stuck in a kind of feedback frustration loop in which old ways of thinking prevented an awareness of the correct creative solution. The experience of the waking mind was a little bit like what sometimes happens to us when we have something "at the tip of our tongue."

Let's say that you've recently met someone named Fisher for the first time. Later, you're having a conversation with someone else and want to tell her about Mr. Fisher, but you can't remember his name. Still, you have the feeling that if you just tried a little harder you could remember it. So you start to make guesses. Now, since you don't remember the name, we might expect that your guesses would be random. You might guess Smith or Jones or Rubinstein or Antonelli. Any old name might come to mind. But that's not what happens when the name is on the tip of your tongue. Your guesses will make sense in that they will be close to the target name. You might guess Foster or Fraser or Farmer or maybe Hunter. All of these guesses are related in some way to the target name you're trying to remember. The first three all start with the same letter as the target. The last one has a meaning similar to the target since both refer to an activity of acquiring food by capturing or killing animals. And all of the guesses, like the target word, have two syllables.

So if you have completely forgotten the name Fisher, why are your guesses so close to the target? The answer, of course, is that the unconscious mind remembers the name Fisher and steers the conscious mind's guesses in the right direction, just as Elias Howe's unconscious mind knew the mechanical key that would unlock the mystery of how to build a working sewing machine.

Recall also Janice's dream of her son toddling across the deck into the swimming pool. That dream revealed that the unconscious mind had gathered and remembered the information that there was something wrong with the lock to the back door. The dream was like a life-saving letter from the unconscious mind to the conscious mind. This letter was a gift that may have saved her son's life.

But still not completely answered is the question of why the unconscious mind sometimes seems to be more observant and smarter than the conscious mind. My take on this question is that the major weaknesses of the unconscious mind can sometimes be its greatest strength. Perhaps that is true for all of us to some degree. If you look at your talents, they often are also your liabilities. If you tend to be well-organized and careful, you may also run the risk of being rigid and lacking in creativity. On the other hand, if you are wonderfully spontaneous and creative, you may also tend to be unpredictable and maybe unreliable.

The title of this book refers to the unconscious mind as *Your Genius Within.* It might have more accurately been titled *Your Savant Within.*

In the 1988 movie *Rainman,* Dustin Hoffman played the role of Raymond Babbitt who was an autistic savant. Raymond could neither perform the usual activities of daily life nor care for himself on his own. Neither could he participate in meaningful and appropriate verbal interactions with the people around him. His capacity to engage with the world was severely limited. Yet he displayed a remarkable ability to remember very specific observations. For instance, he had memorized a large section of the telephone book that he had been looking at in the hotel room where he and his brother were staying. His brother Charlie realized that this memorization skill could be very valuable in Las Vegas if he could get Raymond to apply it to counting cards. This twist in the plot turned out to have a lot of entertainment value for the movie though it was not especially realistic. A real life autistic savant would probably have been overwhelmed by the huge number of distractions in a Las Vegas casino. But still and all, Raymond's amazing memory abilities are not at all far-fetched.

Our unconscious mind is a bit like Raymond's mental capacities. The unconscious mind clearly does not have a very firm grasp on everyday reality. During our dreams, we are usually not smart enough to realize that the bizarre events going on around us are not real. Our language capacity is practically nonexistent. And sometimes, even our dream body's ability to physically move is severely compromised.

In addition, the unconscious mind often seems to have forgotten very obvious details about our life. For instance, even though my parents have been deceased for many years, my unconscious mind often forgets that and continues to think and behave as though they are still living. So insistent is this amnesia that I am totally convinced during my dream that the parents I am having a conversation with are very much alive.

So the sleeping unconscious mind is in many ways not nearly as bright and efficient as the conscious mind. If all we had were the functions displayed by the unconscious mind, we would probably be like Raymond, pretty much unable to cope with daily reality. But the unconscious mind has its savant abilities. The unconscious mind is indeed a regular genius at certain kinds of understanding. As we have seen in the examples above, it can be brilliantly observant and creatively intelligent in certain situations.

Similarly, the conscious mind, while very efficient at getting us through our days relatively unscathed, is often rather stupid when it comes to thinking outside the box and seeing solutions that call for letting go of the usual ways of looking at things. We might say that under the best of circumstances these two parts of our mind make a pretty good team.

I am certainly not the first person to observe, however, that in our modern western society, the unconscious mind is often not given the credit it deserves. Most of us regularly ignore our dream life, which is the major way our unconscious makes itself known to us.

Another method of communication from the unconscious is what we call intuition. And this is often also undervalued. The difference between an insight and intuition lies in how aware we are of how we arrived at a particular solution to a problem. When we have an insight, we are pretty aware of how we got there. An intuition is also the result of internal mental processing. But in the case of intuition, the processing has gone on without our being aware of it. In other words, the problem-solving process has taken place unconsciously. Intuition experiences are, like dreams, often discounted as fuzzy minded and not to be trusted. We might do well to be less dismissive of both of these communications from our inner mind.

Back around 12 paragraphs ago, I referred to a second question that arises from the Elias Howe dream. Namely: Why did the solution to the sewing machine problem appear in such an elaborate and bizarre nightmare where most of the content would seem to be irrelevant to solving the problem?

The answer is that dreams are almost always layered with a number of meanings all being expressed at the same time.

If we employ some of the dream interpretation techniques discussed earlier, we would uncover a whole wealth of meaning in this dream and a good deal of it would turn out to be relevant to the sewing machine issue.

First of all, let's look at the obvious and almost playful symbols that pop up all over the place in this dream. The wide-awake Elias Howe was being consumed or eaten up by the sewing machine problem. So it's no surprise that cannibals would figure prominently in this dream. And just as he was being chased down by the cannibals, he had been trying to chase down a solution to his mechanical stalemate. We might also guess that, since this problem had consumed so much of his time, he would probably be in financial hot water if he did not soon move forward with the project in a way that would turn a profit. Thinking about the problem probably had Howe all tied up in knots. And we then notice that, just before the solution appears, he's able to break free from his confining ropes. And finally, as he was trying to climb out of the cooking pot, the solution was literally beating him over the head as the natives poked and prodded him with their knothole spears.

In spite of the limitations in the intelligence of the unconscious mind, this dream displays its brilliance in bringing so many images together that the dreamer's conscious mind would have to be a total dullard not to get it.

Hypnagogic Dreams

In an earlier chapter, I mentioned that while we are transitioning between being awake and being asleep we pass through a state of consciousness called hypnagogic sleep. Because we are headed for unconsciousness, we usually don't remember the vivid images that frequently occur during this state. But if something awakens us at the right time, the images will often be recalled clearly and in detail.

Hypnagogic dreams seem to be especially rich sources of information about your world. Hypnagogic dreams that inspire and fuel creativity are not unusual.

Salvatore Dali is probably the best-known artist who painted in the surrealist style. The surrealists broke with traditional art and expressed the youthful rebelliousness that followed the disillusionment from World War I. That war has been described as perhaps the most pointless war in history.

Much surrealist art is dreamlike. The paintings often seem to portray a world that does not obey the usual laws of physics. It was as though the artists were rejecting even the physical characteristics of a world that could lead to such senseless horrors. Several surrealist painters, most notably Salvador Dali, revealed that some of their paintings were direct expressions of dreams.

Dali wrote a short manuscript containing advice for aspiring young artists. Much of the advice is playful and perhaps tongue-in-cheek. One of the pieces of advice he gives presents a method for capturing in memory the dreamlike images that flutter through the mind as we doze off. These hypnagogic images were apparently a frequent source of inspiration for Dali. This particular piece of advice was called "slumber with a key". His instructions are for the artist to place a plate upside down on the floor and then sit in a comfortable armchair with a heavy key grasped gently between the thumb and forefinger of his arm resting on the arm of the chair. The key should be positioned such that it is directly above the plate on the floor.

All the young artist has to do is lean back comfortably in the chair and relax. If all goes well, he will enter a state of hypnagogic sleep and after a brief time his fingers will relax and the key will crash into the plate awakening him so that he can recall the images that have been dancing across his mind. These images will provide inspiration for creative work. This technique was especially recommended for those times when an artist feels at a loss to come up with original material.

This extended piece of advice, along with other commentaries written by Dali, suggests that his dream inspirations likely came more often from the hypnagogic state than from rapid eye movement dreams. This seems also to be the case for many creative people, including artists, writers and scientists among others.

It is well-known, for instance, that Thomas Edison was in the habit of not getting much sleep. Instead of a full night of slumber, he often preferred to take catnaps and shared that he would sometimes awaken with fresh ideas concerning the projects he was working on.

Another scientific breakthrough that has been attributed to a dream was the unlocking of the secret of the structure of benzene. This mysterious structure had baffled chemists. While working extensively on this problem, Friedrich Kekule awakened from a dream in which a snake was eating his own tail. He woke up convinced that he had finally discovered the answer to the riddle. Benzene was not structured along a straight line but was contained within a structure that resembled his dream image of a snake eating its own tail.

Kekule reported that his dream occurred to him while he was riding on the upper level of a horse-drawn bus in London. This suggests that it was a hypnagogic dream rather than a rapid eye movement dream.

Hypnagogic images often present creative insights in a fairly straightforward manner. It seems that though the images are a product of unconscious meanderings, they are also under the influence of the conscious mind. This might be called twilight thinking. It has the advantage of having a foot in both worlds so that the insights come from a creative deep place but are filtered through the dreamer's conscious rational mind. Such insights often prove to be very useful.

Rapid eye movement dreams, on the other hand, are usually almost completely under the domination of the unconscious mind. As we have seen, such dreams are fanciful and express themselves in symbols, metaphors, figures of speech and intense imagery. Nonetheless, such dreams, when remembered, can bring meaningful and important creative insights to conscious awareness.

As we saw in the case of Elias Howe, another way in which rapid eye movement dreams differ from hypnagogic dreams is that they bring to the surface a whole bunch of unconscious material in addition to the creative insight that is like the pearl hidden in a batch of oysters.

Dreams That Reveal Your Conscious Mind

Let's move on now to look at dreams in a different way. All of us have things that we wish for. Dreams usually tell us something we are not generally aware of about our wishes. But if we thought about it, we would not be overly surprised. So such dreams tell us about our conscious mind. By that I mean that the dream material is not buried especially deeply in the unconscious mind.

For instance, when I was in college I had a disturbing dream about having an affair with my best friend's wife. I had vaguely been aware of having an attraction to her, but the dream went beyond that awareness. Because of the dream, I was able to guard myself against acting on a wish that could have undermined my friendship. I also began to notice that my friend tended to put me and his wife together in situations that almost seemed like a test. I now was alerted to the importance of passing those tests.

Similarly, dreams of killing somebody might alert you that you have hostility toward this person that you had previously only been partly aware of. Dreams of stealing your boss' car might suggest that you are jealous of his possessions, and, if you're not careful, such jealousy might come to the surface in destructive ways. A dream of a snowstorm preventing you from getting to work might simply be saying that it's about time for a day off.

Sometimes, these dreams might express themselves a bit more indirectly. Jim Hannon had a repetitive dream many times over the years. He was a 58-year-old attorney who worked alone in a moderately successful practice in a small city in upstate New York. The dream was always about him playing high school football again in his hometown in rural Ohio. Although he had not been first-string, he had played frequently. Though he was always a fan of the game, he had not gone on to play football in college. But the dreams of playing again in high school had always baffled him. In some dreams, he was actually out on the field with the team, but most of the time there was an element of frustration. Sometimes, he would be unable to find his uniform while the team was already out on the field. At other times, he was unable to find the location of an away game and was driving around asking for directions. Sometimes, he showed up at the wrong game and discovered that two neighboring teams were playing that day and that his hometown team had an away game somewhere else and it was now too late to get there.

In our dream group, Jim talked about his memories of high school football. And before long, it became obvious that playing on the team was one of last times he'd felt part of a group that worked together for a goal. He had always considered himself a loner, but this dream showed him that there was another side of him that wished expression.

Sigmund Freud believed that all dreams are a kind of wishful thinking. And it seems apparent that Jim Hannon's repetitive dream was just such a dream. The frustrations may very well represent his own reluctance to find a context in which to become a member of a group. Jim was somewhat shy and described his life as pretty solitary. And although he said he liked it that way, the dream seemed to suggest otherwise.

Jim Hannon's dreams tell us that while he does seem to want to reclaim membership in a group, he may also be in conflict about his desire. His dreaming mind keeps setting him up for failure so that we wonder if maybe he wants a kind of togetherness with other people but also fears and even avoids it.

Dreams That Reveal Your Unconscious Mind

So far, we've been talking about pretty straightforward ways of looking at dreams. We've been saying that the first thing to do is to look and see what waking reality is being shown us in the dream. And then the idea is to look and see if there's some kind of semi-conscious wish that is being expressed along with some reluctance about the wish.

A third way of working with dreams is a little trickier. It involves looking at dreams in a symbolic way. In order to get into this deeper level of work, let's start out by looking at Jim's dream in a symbolic manner, since his dream seems to be on the borderline between consciousness and unconsciousness.

Maybe his dreaming of being part of a football team should be looked at as representing something other than what it is. For instance, maybe the football team represents the Bar Association in which he is a member. Upon considering this possibility, Jim confessed that he often feels left behind and out of it in regard to this association. He also said that he intends to get more involved but somehow never gets around to it. He is of an age and has been a member so long that it would be logical for him to have run for office, but that hasn't happened.

So, maybe the dream is saying that he is not showing up for the game and that, if he wants to get more involved, he needs to get dressed in the uniform in a timely fashion. The uniform may be a symbol for wearing the colors so to speak. In other words, maybe he lacks enthusiasm to advocate for his chosen profession. And that lack of enthusiasm is resulting in him not being considered a team player. The dream may be spelling out all of these ideas using the language of symbols.

Janice's dream about the faulty door latch was so clearly about what it was clearly about that it's tempting to not even consider an alternative explanation. But let's say that she had gotten up in the middle of the night and there was nothing wrong with the door. In fact, any attempt to see a danger to her son was a dead-end. So what then? What else might the dream mean?

The first answer is that we don't know for sure. But one way to try to break into the code would be to look at the dream as a kind of symbol for some aspect of Jan's life. Maybe there is a locked door in need of opening. And maybe in the dream, her son Jason gives her a hint as to what needs to happen. His innocence and exuberance may be something that she needs to copy. And maybe his attraction in the dream to a beach ball suggests that being playful might be called for to improve her life. The fact that in the dream she presented a story that had a strong component of danger in it suggests that she may consider her own longing for fun and freedom to be a dangerous impulse.

If it had turned out that Frank's brother Steve had not been in danger of committing suicide, and there was no real-world substance to Frank's concern, then we would look at the dream as maybe a symbol for something in Frank's own life. Maybe Frank was in need of letting go into a kind of death of the old in order to make room for the new. Read psychologically, a dream about death often has to do with the need for change in one's life.

George, a 29-year-old plumber who was engaged to be married, had a disturbing dream in which he was walking across a frozen pond to get to his fiancée on the other side. When he was nearly to the middle, he realized that the ice was too thin to hold him. No sooner had he had that thought when he heard the ice begin to crack and felt himself losing his balance as the ice gave way beneath him. He woke up shivering from having been dumped into the icy water.

George and his fiancée lived in Florida and had no plans to travel north, so the dream was definitely not about actual ice. In working with this dream, George came to the conclusion that the dream was telling him that he was "on thin ice" with his fiancée.

This new awareness led him to check out the situation, and he became increasingly concerned about the status of their relationship. This dream encouraged him to take a second look, and then to proceed with an examination of himself and his fiancée and whether the relationship truly would lead to a happy union. He came to the conclusion that the relationship was worth the effort, and he turned over a new leaf in several aspects of their life together. In fact, he had a second dream in which he was back in high school putting together a leaf collection. And, you guessed it, in the dream he was repeatedly examining and re-examining a leaf specimen first on one side and then the other. This dream gave him a strong confirmation that he had indeed needed to turn over a new leaf.

The Picture Language of Dreams

The above dreams introduce us to the idea that dreams speak to us using a picture language that often puts into images ideas that we usually express in words. This may be because dreams come from a deep place within us where language is not the primary way of thinking. We could speculate that, among our animal friends, this picture language is the main, or maybe the only, way that thinking takes place. Imagine for a moment what kinds of thoughts go through the mind of your pet dog or cat. They don't think in words, so their thinking must be of another kind. It might be accurate to say that they live in a dreamlike world of pictures and images, sounds and feelings. In our dream life, language seems to fall away, leaving us in this same vivid world.

So, when looking to understand your dreams, check out possible picture language in the form of figures of speech that are vividly presented. The following are some examples of dreams from my dream classes and workshops that contain such pictures that express important ideas.

A student of mine had a dream in which he was chasing after a bus that he had missed. Another dreamer was unable to climb a ladder. Another saw himself in bed with his sister nearby. The reason he was in bed was because he was sick and tired. Another dreamer was asleep at the wheel of a bus. Another dreamer had fallen off a wagon. I could go on, but you get the idea.

There are a number of common dream images that appear so often that I'd like to suggest some possibilities for interpretation. Remember, however, that all dreams are individual to the particular dreamer. Any interpretation must be checked out by the dreamer himself. A meaningful interpretation will feel right and make sense to the dreamer. So with that in mind, let's talk about a few common stories or situations that show up in dreams.

A dream that is very frequent is of being unable to move or only being able to move in slow motion. First, since we are all paralyzed during rapid eye movement sleep, this dream might actually be picking up that information and presenting it to us. Second, looking at these dreams as providing information from the waking world, we might speculate that the dreamer is tired or maybe getting sick and the dream presents that idea and should be taken as suggesting a need for more rest or to see a physician. On a slightly deeper level, the dream might be saying that you are stuck in your life in some way and need to get unstuck and maybe make some changes. Or the dream might be saying the opposite. It might be advising that you need to slow down or stay put for a while in spite of your urge to get moving. Again, it's important to remember that the interpretation of the dream is an individual matter related to a person's current life circumstances.

A second common dream experience is of falling. Again, there may be a physical basis for this dream, because the area of the brain that seems to kick off rapid eye movement sleep is very close to the area that brings us our sense of where we are in space at any given moment. This sense is called the *kinesthetic sense* and tells us the position of our body in space. Some people, such as acrobats and gymnasts, have a very well-developed kinesthetic sense. Such people report frequent flying dreams, which may be a kind of improvement over falling dreams because, in this case, you're getting somewhere.

A second interpretation would be to take the dream as providing information from the world. Maybe you're actually in danger of falling because of loose carpeting on a staircase or a faulty guard rail on an outside second-story porch. A third interpretation is to look at falling as a figure of speech. Maybe you have gotten too high and mighty and need to be brought down to earth.

A third common theme is of being lost. During one period of my life, one of my frequent recurring dreams was that I couldn't find my way back home from a visit to a different part of town. If you have this dream, check out the possibility that you've lost your way in some aspect of your life. On the other hand, the dream could be saying that you don't really want to go back home. There may be more adventure and travel in your heart's desires.

Another common image is that of being in public with no clothes on or perhaps in just your underwear. A literal interpretation would be that maybe you need to be careful when you get dressed to make sure you didn't miss anything or put on clothing that is about to fall off. Because that is unlikely, it's probably safe to say that the dream has some kind of symbolic meaning. It could be that you fear that you will soon be exposed for some transgression, real or imagined. Or maybe you already feel too exposed and need to be more careful about whom you share information with or what kind of information. The opposite can also be true. Maybe the dream is a kind of wish that you could be more real or authentic in your public life. Maybe the dream is telling you it's time to let go of your narrowly defined public image.

Many of us dream of being late for an appointment. Sometimes traffic gets in the way, or you may just realize that you had forgotten the appointment and now it's too late to get there on time. Taken literally, the dream might mean that you need to be more careful about your scheduling and that, as a matter of fact, you might be about to miss some important engagements. Or maybe you've been scheduling yourself too tightly so the dream is telling you that, unless you get your act together, this will begin to happen more frequently. A different interpretation suggests that you might be feeling that you've lost some important opportunities in life and that you think it's too late to get them back. The underlying message might be that you could reconsider that conclusion. Maybe upon reflection you'll discover that it's not really too late after all. On the other hand, it could be too late and you are called to accept what you cannot change.

Many of my students and workshop members have reported dreams of losing all or some of their teeth. The first interpretation is to consider going to the dentist to make sure everything in your mouth is all right. If that turns out to be a dead-end, then think of the dream as having something to do with your public image. After all, smiling and showing our teeth are important social conventions. Maybe you need to be more careful about your public image. On the other hand, maybe it's time to consider being more authentic rather than less. Your dream is telling you so by giving you a picture of one possible way of doing so. So take out your teeth, so to speak, and enjoy showing the world what it looks like not to care so much about how you appear.

Having lost or misplaced important items is another common storyline in dreams. Again, a literal interpretation might be to look around and make sure nothing important is missing.

Rachel, who was engaged to be married, dreamed that she had lost her engagement ring. When she woke up from the dream, she checked out her hand and was shocked to realize that she was not wearing the ring. She vaguely remembered absentmindedly slipping it on and off her knuckle while she was in a movie theater the night before. She rushed over to the theater when it opened at 10 a.m. and asked permission to go check around the seat where she had been sitting. After only a brief search, she found the ring. A deeper interpretation would suggest that perhaps she had some mixed feelings about her upcoming marriage plans.

It also could be that a dream of losing something suggests that the dreamer is in danger of losing something more psychological, such as a friendship that might be slipping away. Or the opposite interpretation might be appropriate. Maybe the dream is saying don't hold on so tightly to your possessions or even your relationships but let go, move forward and seize the moment.

Many times, I have dreamed of being back in an earlier period of my life. Sometimes it's my childhood home that is the setting for my dream. Sometimes it's high school or college or the teaching position I used to have before I moved to Florida. Such dreams might be simple nostalgia. Maybe they suggest the importance of looking back and taking stock of where you've been in order to move forward with intelligence and foresight. Or, maybe there is some element of life that was present then that you might want to try to recapture. Or, the opposite interpretation might be true. Maybe the dream is saying that enough is enough, and that looking back is going to only keep you stuck, and it's time to move on. A clue to which of these messages is the one that is accurate is to check out your emotions while having the dream. If returning to an earlier life seems pleasant, that's one thing. If it's a major drag to be back there, that's another.

Multiple Personality Dreams

In working with dreams that reveal your unconscious, it often turns out that there are different parts of yourself that are being expressed that may be in conflict with each other.

In these dreams, there are two or more parts of the inner personality that are in conflict with one another. One character in the dream might be angry, yet another frustrated or disgusted. A basic assumption in these kinds of dreams is that each character in the dream is a different inner personality of the dreamer. So I call these dreams multiple personality dreams. The dreams that yield to this kind of interpretation often involve a kind of inner combat or turmoil. A common such dream is a dream of being chased by somebody or something.

Duncan dreamed of being hunted by a pack of wolves. He lived in the city, so a literal interpretation didn't make much sense. Nether did an interpretation involving wishful thinking seem to him to be the right one. So we went on to discuss the possibility of an inner conflict.

This brings us to an important way of working with dreams. And we will later be talking more about using self-hypnosis to get into this method. But for now, I will give you an idea of how this work goes and how dramatic the results can be in terms of understanding your inner self.

The first thing to be said about these dreams is to understand that each of us is made up of a number of different inner characters. This may seem like a strange thing to say, but I think it will make sense as we proceed.

One way of working with dreams is to try to give the different characters in the dream a chance to speak. In the case of Duncan's dream, we decided in the group to let him take some time and speak to the wolves and let them talk back. The method used to work with dreams this way is sometimes called the *gestalt* method or the empty chair method.

So Duncan was invited to sit comfortably in a chair with an empty chair directly across from him while the other members of the dream group sat in a circle around the two chairs. I instructed Duncan to sit and talk to the other chair as though the wolves were right there with him across the way in the chair. I told them to say whatever he wanted to or ask any questions of the wolves.

Duncan, like most people at first, found these instructions difficult to follow. He said he felt silly and even confessed to the feeling that it would be a waste of time. He said that maybe other people could get into such dramatics, but for him it would just be an act and it would mean nothing. I urged him to begin anyway.

He started by asking the wolves why they were chasing him. He asked the question very matter-of-factly, but since he had been very frightened in the dream, I asked him to ask the question with more emotion. I asked him to repeat the question several times. After he had done so, I instructed him to move to the other chair and try to give voice or words to the wolves and give them permission to talk back to him. He was surprised to hear himself say, as the wolves, "We are chasing you because we are hungry and you never feed us." Duncan changed seats again and said, "But why must you be so ferocious and scare the living daylights out of me?" I asked Duncan to change chairs again and answer as the wolves. They responded, "Because you never listen to us unless we get really nasty. Besides, that's what hungry wolves do."

By now, Duncan had gotten into the swing of things and was moving back and forth from one chair to the other without being told to do so. It was all going swimmingly until Duncan suddenly stopped the conversation and began to cry. In my experience, this is not a turn for the worse but is actually a breakthrough moment of often dramatic significance. Duncan revealed that he had never thought of it this way, but that he'd been terribly neglecting his inner animal self. He didn't quite put it that way, but that was the main point of his insight. The inner warfare was between his very proper and controlled outward personality and his inner, more primitive, even wild, side. During the continuing conversation between himself and the wolves, Duncan came to a kind of resolution that left him feeling excited and energized about the days ahead of him and the choices he would be more likely to make now that he understood that he needed to give some attention to this other part of himself.

Virginia was a 27-year-old freelance writer who often felt a powerful and irresistible urge to procrastinate. She described this as her major fault and said that sometimes weeks would go by without her doing any work. Then, as a writing deadline would approach, she would have to pull several all-nighters in order to get finished on time.

In a dream group, Virginia reported the following vivid dream. She was riding a horse that was a more aged version of a horse she had ridden as a teenager, when she had a summer job at a riding stable near her childhood home. In this dream, she couldn't get the horse to move at anything but a snail's pace. She yelled at it, repeatedly kicked it, and even used a riding crop to try to get the beast to do her bidding. All of this was to no avail. The horse moved along at its own slow pace without seeming to even notice its rider's increasingly shrill attempts to speed it up.

We first took a shot at interpreting the dream as maybe saying something about the real world. But there were no animals in her life during this chapter. So it seemed unlikely that we were talking about a stubborn animal that might need to be dealt with. The idea of a wish fulfillment did not make much sense either. So it was time to move on to the gestalt method.

In our dream group, we set up the two chairs for Virginia to have her dialogue. Like Duncan, she said that she had little confidence that the conversation would yield anything and asked if maybe we could think of another way to get to understand this dream. She was sure she would find the whole thing exceedingly embarrassing and her self-consciousness would prevent any good work from being done. But after some coaxing, she was willing to at least give it a try. So with Virginia in one chair and the stubborn horse in the other, the conversation began. As in most of these conversations, it started out with a simple question. Virginia asked the horse, "Why do you have to move so slowly?" She didn't seem to have anything more to say so I asked her to move to the other chair and answer as the horse. The horse said simply, "Because I want to." Then back to the other chair. "Why'd you have to be so stubborn and always walk at a slow pace? You frustrate me so much, and you act as though you're not even paying attention to me. I've tried everything I know how to do to get you to get going." Virginia sat in the horse's chair for several minutes, seemingly drawing a blank regarding what to say next. Then the light bulb seemed to go on and she started responding as the horse. "You have no idea how much it hurts me when you kick and slap and hit and scream at me. You don't ever ask me if I need to rest or where I might want to go. You just try to bully me into giving you your way." I could see that Virginia was beginning to get into this conversation as she moved back to her own chair again. "It never occurred to me to ask you where you want to go. After all, horses are supposed to go where their riders take them." Then the horse spoke again. "But I'm not just any horse. I'm your horse and I have a mind of my own, and if you don't listen to me you're not going to get anywhere." Virginia responded, "I'm sorry I haven't been listening. I had no idea you have an opinion in the matter. What is it you want to do? Where would you like to go?" The horse replied, "I certainly don't want to go on the boring monotonous rides that you have been taking lately. And you always take me over dry land with no water to drink and no grass to eat. So I end up hungry, thirsty and bored."

Virginia could no longer contain herself. She said she wanted to talk about what this all meant and what this conversation was really about. She had been taking freelance work that paid well but gave her no pleasure. She knew that there was other work out there that would excite her, but it wouldn't pay the bills, so she was forcing herself to plod through the work. But, sometimes, she just couldn't force herself and ended up procrastinating for long periods of time.

The dream about the stubborn horse brought to light a conflict within her. One part of her legitimately demanded that she do work that would bring her financial security. Another part of her wished to fulfill the valued goal of doing satisfying and creative work. She had been letting the practical part of herself completely dominate her choices. The suppressed creative energies were resorting to procrastination in retaliation. Clearly, a new accommodation and compromise was called for. She later told me that she went home and continued the dialogue with the horse, who gave her some really good ideas about how to proceed. Her professional life took a dramatic turn for the better.

As we work with our dreams, we are working on the deepest parts of ourselves. There is lots of scientific evidence that REM sleep plays an important role in helping us maintain and improve our mental and emotional health. For instance, patients who have been regularly getting a good night's sleep seem to do better in their ongoing psychotherapy than patients who are sleep-deprived. There is something about REM sleep especially that helps a person integrate both the ideas and the positive emotions that they've learned in therapy. So dreaming helps a person to transfer important progress from the therapeutic work into everyday life. This is quite remarkable and shows that there is a lot going on during our dreams that is important to how we live and feel during the day.

My website, www.hypnosisdreams.com, provides a forum for conversations about dreams and ways of working with them.

Many people believe that one of the things going on during dreams is extrasensory perception. In the next chapter, we turn our attention to that topic.

Chapter 17

ESP

What if you slept? And what if, in your sleep, you dreamed? And what if, in your dream, you went to heaven and plucked a strange and beautiful flower? And what if, when you awoke, you had the flower in your hand? Ah, what then?
Samuel Taylor Coleridge

In the spring of 2011, an article that appeared in one of the most prestigious and trusted scientific journals in the field of psychology caused a huge uproar among psychology researchers in the United States and around the world. The article reported on a research study testing the possibility of accurate precognitions. A *precognition* is knowing what will happen in the future.

There is no scientific way to explain how this could possibly happen. So research studies suggesting that such things exist have been dismissed by the scientific community by saying that any such findings are impossible because they defy any explanation. The conclusion, then, is that the results must have been achieved through either random luck or the dishonesty of researchers.

So when Prof. Daryl Bem of Cornell University, who has had impeccable research credentials for over 40 years, published positive results about precognition, the scientific community was shocked. His article was published in *The Journal of Personality and Social Psychology*, a mainstream publication of the American Psychological Association. The journal is so strict in screening out questionable research that it rejects over 80 percent of submissions from scientists around the world.

In a response to one of the many critics who attacked his findings even before they appeared in the Journal, Prof. Bem pointed out that, using the best and most current statistical methods, the probability that his results were due to chance was about seventy billion to one.

I want to be quick to add that Prof. Bem's study is not about people predicting train wrecks, the death of a public figure or any such events. Instead, this study focused on very specific and limited situations in which hundreds of research subjects produced results on tasks where they were instructed to make certain guesses. The way the study was set up, subjects were given choices between two alternatives with no hints or information that should have given them better than a 50-50 chance of being right. It turned out that, under certain circumstances, subjects were right over 53 percent of the time. Now, that may not seem like a high number, but it is more than enough to be significant. To be cautious about it, however, it should be pointed out that subjects were wrong almost 47 percent of the time. So whatever is going on is not especially consistent.

In 1921, Sigmund Freud wrote to a friend saying, "I do not belong with those who reject in advance the study of so-called occult phenomena as being uncertain, unworthy or harmful." In 1924, Freud apparently wanted to present a paper in support of the validity of mind-to-mind telepathy at a psychoanalytic conference. Freud was talked out of presenting the paper by those who said that his controversial ideas were already unbelievable to many, and so to add this new twist could destroy the psychoanalytic movement. Freud gave in and did not present the paper, which was finally published about 20 years later, after his death.

Freud was not alone in his assertion of the worthiness of the study of psychic phenomena. Carl Jung came to a similar conclusion based on a lifetime of studying the human mind.

I have opened this chapter with support for taking psychic phenomena seriously from a number of heavyweights in the fields of psychology. I have done this as a response to the voices of the vast majority of psychology researchers and practitioners who scoff at such reports, as that of Francine, which I retold in the preamble to this book. Francine is convinced that she had a vivid and realistic precognitive dream about the attack upon her twin sister. The critics describe such reports as the products of wishful thinking combined with memory distortions, or as just made up. While it is true that many such reports can be accurately characterized in this manner, I believe that this is not always the case. There are some reports that seem to defy our capacity to understand them.

The terms *parapsychology*, *psychic phenomena*, or *extra-sensory perception* are used differently by different writers. But the overlapping labels refer to phenomena that are as elusive and difficult to pin down as they are fascinating and important to study. The most common of these terms is extrasensory perception (ESP).

The term extrasensory perception describes experiences that are extra-sensory, meaning beyond our sensory capacity to perceive. For instance, our eyes, which are capable of perceiving within certain limits, cannot see through walls. Neither can they physically see what is going on 1,000 miles away. So if I claim to see something that my eyes just can't see, I am making a claim for extrasensory perception.

There are three kinds of extra-sensory experiences that have been claimed and studied. The first, called *telepathy*, is essentially mind-to-mind communication. There is no physical perceptual mechanism by which I can read your mind. So if I claim to do so, I am making a claim for mental telepathy. The second kind of ESP is *clairvoyance*, which is the perception of remote events. So if I claim that I see or have seen a train wreck that happened thousands of miles away, I am making a claim for clairvoyance. The third kind of ESP is *precognition*, which is the perception of events before they happen. So if I claim that I saw your car accident before it happened, I am making a claim for precognition.

Over the years, I have gotten used to members of my classes or dream groups talking about all three kinds of extra-sensory perception occurring in their dreams. For some people, such experiences seem to be a regular occurrence and often involve relatively trivial events, like predicting that a certain relative is going to call on the phone. For others, the experience is a once-in-a-lifetime event, usually very dramatic. Telepathic experiences are usually the most emotionally charged, such as dreaming that a loved one is in intense emotional distress and then having that turn out to be the case.

I used to try to steer dream group members in the direction of interpreting such dreams as being the result of the sleeping mind creating a dream from information that had been perceived during the previous day using the usual senses. Examples of this kind of interpretation are the dreams of Janice and Frank from an earlier chapter. You may recall that Janice had what turned out to be a warning dream about the danger of her child drowning in her pool. Frank's dream was about his brother's suicide. In both cases, the dreams seem to be woven from information from waking life. I have discovered over the years, however, that these kinds of explanations only account for a portion of these kinds of dreams. Many dreamers find such explanations unsatisfying and not credible.

Dream sharing, in which two people report having the same or almost the same dream during the same night's sleep, is a particular form of telepathy that is sometimes reported in dream groups. These experiences almost always seem to occur when the two people are very close and one or the other of them is going through an emotionally turbulent time.

So here is the question that stands in the background when discussing these kinds of experiences: Is it the case that the sleeping brain can give and receive information from the outside world in ways that are beyond normal sensory experience? Or, is it the case that such experiences result from some kind of brain event that tricks the dreamer into later remembering the dream in a distorted fashion?

There are two widely researched and closely related experiences in regard to which these same questions are crucial. Those are *out-of-body experiences* (OBE) and *near-death experiences (NDE)*.

We know that some people while asleep have the experience of their consciousness somehow leaving their body, and perceiving their body and sometimes other things in the environment, from an outside perspective. We also know that somewhere between 10 and 20 percent of patients who have experienced cardiac arrest have had some sort of near-death experience in which they leave their body and have experiences from what seems like a different level of reality.

Most of the research regarding both of these experiences has centered on trying to locate where in the brain such experiences are generated. There have been some successes in these research efforts, and some critics interpret those successes as meaning that the experiences are simply the result of an overstressed brain playing tricks on us. This kind of explanation generally leaves people who have had first-hand experiences unconvinced.

Research that has attempted to correlate out-of-body experiences with actual events in the surrounding environment --- such that the person, for instance, was able to accurately say what was going on in the next room to which he claims to have traveled --- have been unsuccessful in well-controlled experimental studies.

So what are we to make of all this? My own take is that putting all of the dreamlike experiences together creates a picture of the sleeping mind as actively engaged with many levels of reality. This is clearly the experience of many people who pry open the door between waking consciousness and sleeping consciousness. And sometimes, as in the case of Francine, the connection between such an experience and the external world seems startlingly firm and accurate. Beyond that, I can't say. But I will say that walking back and forth between these two experiential worlds enriches the lives of those who do it.

I would now like to turn our attention to the research and practice of possible psychic perceptions in an unexpected institution. *Remote viewing* is an alternate term used for clairvoyance in a United States Army intelligence project, called the Stargate project, which was in existence from the mid-1970s through 1995. It had a budget of about a half a million dollars a year and was based at Fort Meade, Maryland. At one point, there were apparently as many as a dozen so-called viewers on staff. In 1984, one of the viewers was awarded a Legion of Merit for apparently accurately seeing over 100 different intelligence elements of value that had not been accessible through standard intelligence operations.

The project was eventually moved from Army intelligence to the CIA. In early 1995, the CIA hired the prestigious American Institute of Research to review the procedures and results of the project over the years. Although the Institute concluded that ultimately the project was not providing information of value to the intelligence community, one of its findings was that some viewers scored between 5 and 15 percent above chance in their viewings. In other words, the conclusion was that, in some cases at least, certain individuals seem to have had measurable clairvoyant talents.

The word *premonition* is more commonly used than the term precognition but essentially means the same thing. There have been a number of efforts to register or document premonitions so that there would be evidence of their validity. One such effort did seem to produce some positive evidence.

In one dramatic example, the Central Premonitions Registry in New York City received a telegram predicting that President Reagan would be shot and, if there was no explosion, he would survive the assassination attempt. This prediction, which was received before the March 1981 attempt on Mr. Reagan's life, was based on a precognitive dream which included the information that three to six shots would be fired.

The Central Premonitions Registry was established by Stanley Krippner and Robert Nelson in 1968. Dr. Krippner was the research director at the dream laboratory in the Maimonides Medical Center in Brooklyn, NY. Mr. Nelson was on the staff of the New York Times. The registry was founded during a turbulent time in American history. The 1960s witnessed the assassinations of John F. Kennedy, Martin Luther King and Robert Kennedy. There were many people who reported that they had had premonitions or precognitions about these events. But without advance evidence, the validity of these reports could not be demonstrated.

The two founders shared an interest in the phenomena of precognitive dreams and decided to create the registry to document their validity. Specific requirements had to be met in order for a premonition to qualify for filing. A premonition had to be about a public event; it had to be put in writing; and it had to arrive at the Registry before the event it predicted occurred. Also, the event predicted had to be described in enough detail so as to reasonably rule out coincidence

In 1982, the registry reviewed the results of 14 years of research, which confirmed that the vast majority of premonitions occur in the course of precognitive dreams. As of 1982, a total of 53 premonitions turned out to be accurate. Since mail-in premonitions were received at the Registry at the rate of several thousand per year, it is clear that accurate premonitions, from dreams or otherwise, are a very rare occurrence.

Interestingly, about half of the 53 accurate premonitions came from the same six people. Certain individuals seem to display a special ability in this regard. The highest score earned was by an individual with an accuracy rate of about 10 percent. By the mid-1980s, the registry had dropped out of existence

In 1967, the British Premonitions Bureau was founded in England. It was established right after a coal mining-related disaster in Aberfan, Wales in which 116 children and 28 adults were killed when a saturated mountain of coal mining waste broke loose from the area of the mine and avalanched down the hill into a school and nearby houses. Following the disaster, there were many reports of people who had what they considered precognitive dreams before the event occurred. A psychiatrist named Barker investigated these claims and found at least 16 of them to be well-corroborated. It became clear to him, however, that to be taken seriously such claims would need to be made before the event predicted actually occurred. So he founded the premonitions registry in an attempt to both validate such premonitions and to perhaps avert disasters in the future by heeding the warnings contained in premonitions. The registry existed for about a decade and seems to have left no records of its successes or failures.

As mentioned earlier, telepathy is defined as the sending or receiving of information through non-sensory means, (mind-to-mind communication). Anecdotal accounts of occurrences abound, and many of them are reported to occur during dreams. We might speculate that the mind is especially sensitive to incoming information during the attentiveness that dream sleep involves.

In the early 1970s, a team of researchers at the Maimonides Medical Center in Brooklyn, NY conducted a number of experiments in which dreamers who had previously reported such experiences were mentally sent information by a group of senders who were staring at a photographic slide in a room some distance away. While the researchers report the results to be inconsistent, some of the dreams of receivers seemed to have been influenced by the content of the slide. The research was done very carefully to attempt to rule out various kinds of contamination of the results. This research is described in the 2003 book *Dream Telepathy Experiments in Nocturnal Extrasensory Perception* by Montague Ullman and Stanley Krippner.

Before we wrap up our discussion of extrasensory perception, I would like to mention a haunting experience that over two-thirds of Americans report having had at least once. Déjà vu translated into English means "already seen." It is the experience of feeling certain that a situation that one is experiencing for the first time has happened before. People will say for instance, that they knew in a conversation what was going to be said next. Or they report that they knew what was around the corner in a new city before they got to that spot.

Most people report that as the déjà vu experience was unfolding, they had a strange and somewhat disturbing experience of familiarity and strangeness as though they were in touch with mysterious forces. Many people who experience déjà vu interpret their experience as being related to precognition. Unlike most claims of precognition, however, this one has unfolded in reverse. In the mind of the believer in ESP, the current déjà vu experience is the result of having previously had a precognition of what is taking place at the déjà vu moment. In other words, today's déjà vu is the result of having had a precognitive experience yesterday, or perhaps last night, in a dream.

There is a second interpretation of déjà vu that many people find compelling. According to the second idea, one is remembering an experience from a past life. This explanation is more likely to be believed by those who have experiences such as a strong feeling of familiarity in a city that they never visited before. Some international tourists have this kind of experience often.

In a 2005 Gallup poll, 41percent of Americans said they believe in extrasensory perception and 20 percent believe in some form of reincarnation. So for many people, these kinds of explanations for déjà vu are not a stretch.

The explanation that is more acceptable to the scientific community is that, in one way or another, the mind is playing tricks on us.

One such interpretation sees the experience as a result of an odd misfire in the two human memory systems. We all have a short-term memory which holds information for maybe 20 minutes to a couple of hours or so. This memory system enables us to have meaningful conversations, play cards, watch a sporting event, navigate our way down a road and so on. Long-term memory is the second kind, and this enables us to remember at least certain events from years or even decades ago.

The usual order of memory establishment is that material is first stored in short-term memory and then some of it is later transferred into long-term memory.

The explanation of déjà vu is that somehow a current situation is stored into long-term memory first and then a few seconds later finds its way back to short-term memory. In this way, it feels as though the new memory is really an old memory.

In this chapter, we have explored a variety of topics related to extrasensory perception (ESP). There are no simple answers to the questions raised that will satisfy everyone. But that is perhaps as it should be, for we are talking about experiences on the edge of our consciousness. Just as dreams seem mysterious and otherworldly, so do the experiences that fall outside of our usual perceptions.

My website, www.hypnosisdreams.com, provides a forum for people to discuss their dream experiences that they believe demonstrate extrasensory perception.

In the next chapter, we will talk about how to improve and strengthen the transfer of insight and growth from your dreams into your waking life. The chapter will begin with a dramatic example of how one student in a class I taught at a maximum security prison used the knowledge he had gained in class to actually transform a dream in such a way that it brought him emotional release and satisfaction. He later said that working with this dream did a great deal to help him better adjust to prison life. We will then discuss the ideas and techniques presented in that class and in my dream groups to help you profit from this kind of work.

Chapter 18

The Transformation of a Dream

The Kitty Genovese murder is one of the most famous homicides of the 20th century. Kitty Genovese was a 28-year-old woman who was attacked by a man named Winston Moseley while walking the 30 feet between her car and her apartment building door at 3:15 a.m. on March 13, 1964. A New York Times investigative article revealed that almost 40 neighbors had heard or seen some or all of the attack, which took over a half-hour to unfold, with the attacker fleeing twice only to return and continue his assault, finally murdering and raping his victim.

No one intervened to help.

Social psychologists developed theories and did research regarding the nature of the bystander lack of intervention that night. As a result, there is a phenomenon called the Genovese effect, or the bystander effect. Briefly, the idea is that the more people a bystander thinks are in a position to help, the less likely that bystander is to intervene. In this case, that effect, or maybe just plain apathy, resulted in a needless death.

What follows is a dream reported by Tyron, a student in my psychology class at the New York State maximum security prison in Auburn, NY. It contains the seeds of a technique you can use to transform your dream life.

"I am suddenly startled awake by a bloodcurdling scream," Tyron reported. "I recognize the voice of Kitty Genovese, though in reality I've never heard her voice. She screams, 'He stabbed me, he stabbed me. Oh my God, he stabbed me.' I am certain that her voice is coming from the stairwell at the end of the cell block and I am baffled about how she got into this secure and guarded area. I know instantly that her attacker is Winston Moseley and that he intends to murder her and then rape her as she is dying.

"I can't seem to wake myself up enough to get moving. Her screams have stopped. But I know that this brief intermission will be replaced by more screams, only this time muffled with the sound of bubbling blood in her throat. I will myself with all my might to sit up and then slowly pull myself to my feet by bracing myself against the sink.

"I try the door of my cell, and it is, of course, closed and locked securely. But it occurs to me to try to push a portion of the containment bars directly outward into the catwalk. The bars give way just as I begin to hear Winston also exiting his cell, where he had gone to change hats before returning to resume his pleasure with his victim whose labored breathing I can hear in the distance.

"I figure I have a shot at intercepting this bastard as he passes by my cell. But I can't seem to get myself to move in anything other than extreme slow motion. Meanwhile, I see him casually walk by with a smile on his face and a sideways glance at me that says 'there is nothing you can do about this you pathetic little man.'

"I'm aware that lots of other inmates can hear what's going on but seem not to care. I'm getting more and more infuriated and frustrated and begin to scream. The sound of my own screaming starts to take effect on my awareness, and I begin to wake up only this time for real.

"My T-shirt is soaked and people in adjoining cells are cursing because I have awakened them with yet another of my nightmares.

"As I begin to come to myself, I realize that I am already sitting up in my bunk. I lie back down and start to fall asleep and then remember that my psychology professor had given us a phrase to recite while going to sleep and I couldn't remember it. So I get up and look through my notes and find it and read it aloud to myself. 'I welcome the wisdom of my inner mind.' I then go back into bed and repeat the phrase 20 times using the self-hypnosis technique that our professor had taught us.

"I don't remember finishing the exercise. The next thing I knew I was back in the dream again. Only this time, my cell door was already wide open and the whole place was bathed in warm, almost pink, light. Winston was about to cross in front of my cell when I leapt to my feet and charged him with all my might, catching him and lifting him into the air. After impact, we sailed out across the open space at the center of the cell block. Rather than falling, we remain aloft, but not exactly floating, because the momentum of my leap kept us moving. But I could change directions at will with him in my embrace.

"I began to feel contaminated by Winston's presence, so I simply let go and he crashed to the floor, breaking into many pieces like an empty water glass.

"As I flew around the cell block, I silently communicated with the other inmates and got their cooperation in an effort to help poor Kitty Genovese. Soon, somehow I knew that we had been successful. She was alive and recovering at her mother's house in Connecticut, far from Kew Gardens New York where I knew she had been attacked, even though this dream attack took place here in prison in Auburn, NY.

"Finally, I heard the voice of Billy Graham saying, 'May the Lord bless you real good.' At that point, I woke up again but felt peaceful and blessed and ready for a new day; ready for a new day of blessings, even if I was still an inmate at a maximum security prison."

Tyron, the student inmate who reported this dream, had heard of the case even before we discussed it in a class I taught in the 1980's. He had never met Winston Moseley, who at that time was an inmate in another facility in the New York State prison system. But a number of other members of the class reported having met him at some point during their incarceration. One of the students claimed to have had a fairly close personal relationship with Winston. The student said he had actually spoken with him about this case. The story he told in class, that Winston was amazed that he was able not only to return twice and finally finish off his victim, but that he was able to spend some time cutting off her underwear with his knife and raping her before he casually walked back to his car and left. This other student reported that, rather than being remorseful, Winston was proud of his celebrity status and even said he had done a service to society by furthering the social psychological knowledge that has been gained. Talk about a warped mind.

Dream Incubation

There is more to the point of describing the Kitty Genovese murder case and Tyron's dream about it than just the interesting aspects of the case. My primary reason for discussing it is to use it as an example of how you can transform your dream life even while you're dreaming.

In the prison class and in my dream groups, I talk about techniques to get right into your dreams and learn from them and even transform them. In these ways, we can help our dreams help us more fully.

To understand what I'm talking about, I want to describe a technique that has been around for thousands of years. The technique is called dream incubation, and a form of it was part of the rituals in the many sleep temples that existed in the ancient world.

In the ancient world, the technique involved repeating certain incantations and prayers in order to have a dream that would answer questions about a particular subject or problem. The potential dreamer would then sleep in the sleep temple, and the next day the dreams that came to him that night would be interpreted as answers to the questions that were asked.

There were many sleep temples, also called dream temples, in ancient Egypt around 4,000 years ago. In these places, a lot of therapeutic techniques were used that we would now call hypnosis. But a mainstay of the treatment involved patients gaining insight and being given remedies in their dreams.

These sleep temples and others in Greece and later Rome might be called general hospitals because a wide range of illnesses and techniques to treat them were utilized on large numbers of people.

What we would now term dream incubation was an important part of the treatment regime. These techniques became popular among many early Christian sects and are still practiced in some Greek Orthodox monasteries. The following Scripture passage is sometimes quoted by those who believe that God may still speak to us in dreams.

"Hear now my words: If there be a prophet among you, I the Lord will make myself known unto him in a vision, and will speak unto him in a dream" (Num. 12:6).

The first dream incubation technique you will learn here is based on the self-hypnosis techniques that you learned in chapters 6 and 7. In chapter 6, you learned how to give yourself a simple post-hypnotic suggestion each night before going to sleep by repeating a phrase 20 times. That technique works very well to encourage your awareness of what your sleeping unconscious mind has to say about a particular issue or problem. The technique also works well, as my student discovered, if you wake up from a troubling or especially negative dream and wish to invite your unconscious mind to bring you a more positive dream that will help you to resolve the negative emotions and thinking that are troubling you.

In the case of the Kitty Genovese dream, the inmate at first had a dream that contained a great deal of frustration and feelings of powerlessness in the face of sadistic violence. It is understandable that an inmate in a maximum security prison would have such a dream, which pretty clearly depicts what life can be like on a daily basis there. Tyron woke up deeply disturbed by the dream and his feeling of being pathetic and impotent to combat the evil that he felt so deeply existed in this dream and in the world around him. He woke up enough to begin to repeat a phrase he had learned in class: "I welcome the wisdom of my inner mind." Apparently, this phrase stimulated in him some of his most positive inner strengths of ingenuity and generosity, and his unconscious mind created a revision of the dream that was satisfying, energizing and even transformative.

I'm not so naïve as to suggest that a single dream alone would change a person's life. Probably Tyron had been doing work on his own, and then the work in class culminated in his being able to use this dream to shift his perspective in a way that did have a profound effect upon his life in prison.

So, if you'd like to try dream incubation, you can use the self-hypnotic techniques learned earlier and create some phrases to say at bedtime that might help you encourage your dream work in a positive direction. Some general phrases where you might start work are: "I welcome and remember my dreams," and the one mentioned above: "I welcome the wisdom of my inner mind."

My website, www.hypnosisdreams.com, provides information about and discussions of dream incubation and people's experiences with it.

You might have specific issues you want to work on, and you can design a positive phrase to help take you there in your dreams. One way of asking is to use the phrase: "I welcome dreaming about my work, or my marriage, or my child, or my finances, etc." So pick a topic and ask your dreaming mind to dip into its inner reservoir of wisdom and bring up some helpful material for you to look at. Always remember, however, that your unconscious mind has a wisdom of its own and may not comply with your request immediately. It may have other things on its mind that take priority. But sometimes, your unconscious mind will respond with dreams that bring insightful and important responses to your incubation.

You can also use the indirect suggestions techniques described in chapter seven. My website also offers ideas and possible indirect suggestions stories for you to use.

If you decide to proceed on your own, make up a story that refers indirectly to the problem you're having or the issue you're dealing with.

Tell yourself that story before going to sleep at night, every night for a few nights, and your sleeping mind may pick up the thread of the story and carry it forward in new and creative ways for you to look at. Give it a try. The results can be dramatic.

If you really want to get into using dreaming incubation, the following is a step-by-step set of instructions for asking for dreams that might help you solve or gain new insight into a personal problem or an intellectual challenge.

1. Take the usual steps to encourage dream recall. These steps were presented in chapter 16.
2. Take any objects that might be related to the problem into the bedroom with you. For instance, if you wish to incubate a dream about a love relationship, take a photo of your loved one and place it on your nightstand. If an intellectual problem is what you're working on, you could create a collage or other objects related to the problem and take them to bed with you.
3. Write out the nature of the problem to be addressed. Write it out in as much detail as you'd like.
4. Look over what you've written and boil the problem down so that it can be expressed in a sentence or two. Then copy those sentences on to a 3x5 card or a piece of paper and place it by your bed.
5. Before getting into bed, read over your 3x5 card at least 10 times.
6. Climb into bed and let whatever images you have about the problem wander through your head for a while. Keep yourself from falling asleep during this process.
7. Clearly and directly tell yourself that you will have a dream about this issue. Repeat this idea as many times as you'd like and ideally drift off to sleep in the process.
8. When you wake up, immediately ask yourself if you've been dreaming. Even if you haven't been dreaming, write down whatever comes to mind whether or not your recalled dreams seem to be related to the topic.
9. Thank your dreaming mind for the dream, and ask that more dreams occur when you go back to sleep.

Lucid Dreaming

There is a level of consciousness that we sometimes experience in our dreams that can also be useful in helping us gain as much as possible from them and their access to our inner wisdom. This level of consciousness is called lucid dreaming. When you have a lucid dream, you become aware that you are dreaming while you're still in the dream. Most of us have had this experience occasionally, if only fleetingly. There have been books and articles written about how to encourage lucid dreaming with the idea that such experiences can help us to get the most out of our dreams by, not just remembering them, but experiencing them consciously at the time of dreaming.

One way to increase your chances of becoming lucid during your dreams is to practice being lucid while you are awake. By that I mean that from time to time during the day get in the habit of asking yourself whether you are wide awake or dreaming at that moment. In fact, you can practice this technique right now. Look around the room and ask yourself if everything is obeying the normal laws of physics. For instance, does the table beside you feel solid? Is the light from the lamp or coming through the window the right color and brightness? Now get up out of your chair and walk around the room. Does the floor beneath your feet feel the way it usually does? Look at a clock and see if the hands are slowly moving as they should and if the clock is showing the correct time.

The idea of practicing this technique is that, if you ask yourself these kinds of questions during the day, you will prime yourself to ask these questions while you're dreaming. And when you ask these questions while dreaming, you will often discover that the usual laws of physics are being violated and that your environment in other ways seems strange. These kinds of observations will often lead to you becoming aware that you are dreaming.

The bedtime self-hypnosis technique that by now has become familiar to you can also be used to encourage yourself to be lucid during your dreams. A phrase you might use is: "I will become more aware while I'm dreaming." This general suggestion does not try to force your sleeping mind into becoming lucid but instead makes a general suggestion about awareness that your sleeping mind can interpret and respond to in a manner that suits its best intentions. It is always a good idea to trust the wisdom of our inner minds and not try to be too heavy-handed in our conscious efforts to influence our dreams. Our priority is to listen and to be alert to what we are being taught from this inner wellspring. But there are advantages to being lucid. From that lucid place, we are more likely to remember our dreams and also to understand our dreams from the inside. So give this effort a try and, if it helps, continue to use the process.

My website, www.hypnosisdreams.com. provides more information about and a forum for the discussion of lucid dreaming.

Another way of expanding your understanding of your dreams is by inducing a state of self-hypnosis, and then working with dreams while in that state. This practice can dramatically enhance your work. Here is one way to proceed.

Before using the daytime self-hypnosis technique in chapter 6, open your dream journal to the dream you want to work on. Then do the self-hypnosis. While in the state of self-hypnosis, let your mind wander in the memory of the dream. Write down the associations that come to mind. You may be surprised at how productive this practice can be.

To take this technique even further, you might try using your imagination to continue the storyline of the dream. While in self-hypnosis, pretend that you are asleep and dreaming and see if you can get the dream to continue in your mind. This could be a way of more deeply understanding your dream mind by activating your waking imagination.

Chapter 19

Dreams Through the Stages of Life

Dreams help us to deal with the issues that are the most pressing for us during our current stage of life. The dreams of children are likely to speak to their issues, while the dreams of the elderly address the challenges of the sunset years.

Children often dream about their teachers and their classrooms. Dreams of being chased suggest children's awareness of how vulnerable and dependent they are. Being blamed or punished is a common theme. A common dream situation is of being stuck in a high place and in danger of falling and then falling and waking up on the way down. By the way, most dreamers wake up before hitting the ground, but some don't and survive to tell the story. Dreaming of being lost or unable to find the way home reflects a still incomplete awareness of surroundings.

Children quickly pick up on the idea that dreams can be looked at symbolically. One child for instance said, "No wonder I dreamed of being outside in my underwear. I have to talk in front of the class tomorrow."

Young children are open and eager to share their dreams. Giving children some basic ways of understanding dreams can go a long way toward relieving them of the anxieties that they may have concerning their dreams. For instance, sharing with children that a dream of being chased by a monster is probably related to having been scared during the previous day can be of comfort. Children sometimes take such dreams literally and are concerned that there really is something to be afraid of. With a little help, the child might remember that an adult was grumpy or irritable that day and the monster dream is a good way to get the resulting feelings out.

If you are a parent or caregiver of young children, you can make a contribution to their mental well-being by inviting conversations about dreams. Sharing some of your own dreams sets a good example. But it is most important to be interested in the children's dreams. That way, they get the idea that their inner mind is communicating valuable and interesting information.

Working with older children and teenagers in dream groups is also rewarding. They are usually enthusiastic about sharing their dreams. In our culture, which is dominated by competitiveness and materialism, there are very few contexts in which to discuss one's inner life. Young people generally do not share their dreams with others. In my experience this is not because they don't find dreams interesting and meaningful but because they think other people might think they're strange for talking about dreams.

Nightmares are a normal part of children's dream life. Many people still remember vivid childhood nightmares many decades later. Although negative emotions such as fear or anger appear in our dreams at all ages, they are especially common during our younger years. This is probably because dreams are helping children accomplish the task of dealing with and learning to control their emotions.

Many of the breakthrough dreams of creative people take the form of nightmares. It seems as though the sleeping mind dresses important insights in the clothing of intense emotions in order to get our attention and force us to remember.

Childhood is also the time in life when what Carl Jung called "big dreams" often occur. Big dreams contain archetypical content and have powerful psychological and cultural images and meanings. Most of our dreams are what he called "little dreams," which are concerned with our personal issues of the day. As with nightmares, people sometimes remember childhood big dreams for the rest of their lives. Carl Jung himself talks about how a dreamed image of God deeply affected him throughout his adult life.

College students are still near the beginning of their life journey. Engaging with the world around them and finding their place in it is their life task during this time. Common dream themes that reflect this stage are things such as searching for a certain address, missing a train or airplane, flying through the air and having magic powers.

College students have recently lost their comfortable childhood life. So there are often dreams that express nostalgia, such as encountering a childhood friend and being glad to see him, being back home with family and maybe being reunited with a childhood pet. Dreams of being in airports, train stations or gas stations suggest concerns with moving forward, getting ahead and traveling through life.

Not surprisingly, adults busy with work life and family responsibilities have dreams of being on vacation. While no substitute for the real thing, a dream vacation may be better than nothing. Young adults also have dreams of rescuing people, disciplining children or training pets. These themes reflect the important tasks of caregiving that demand attention during waking life.

In my experience, the dreams of retired persons are often filled with images and experiences of being lost. In one group of eight seniors, all of them had recently remembered such dreams. One man had a repetitive dream in which he was back working at his previous job but could not find his way around the warehouse. Things had been changed around and he just could not figure it all out. A retired schoolteacher reported that in a series of dreams she couldn't find her classroom and was frustrated because she knew she was already late.

Our later years are a time when we are called upon to do some letting go. Retirement for many people turns out to be experienced as a loss. Most people put on a happy face, and there are often many things to celebrate, but dreams can lead us into an honest conversation about facing the accumulating good-byes that pile up on us as the years go by.

In addition to bringing up difficult issues, dreams can contain the seeds of solving them. The gentleman who dreamed of being confused in an old familiar warehouse remembered while reporting the dream to the group that there were some new windows in the warehouse. He then came up with the idea that, next time he had the dream, he would try looking out the windows to see what the scenery was like. Another member of the group then offered that maybe the dream was suggesting that he take the time to look out the window while awake and appreciate the world.

I hope that this little discussion of the relationship between dreams and the various stages of life has been helpful. Being aware of the age related themes of dreams can help us to sort out their meanings.

How do the dreams of imprisoned criminals differ from our own? And do mathematical geniuses dream in the language of math, or are their dreams like those of the rest of us?

In the next chapter, we will discuss these and other examples of how our interests, life passions and current situations can show up in our dreams.

Chapter 20

The Dreams of Prisoners and Mathematicians

Many years ago, I was a student in a fascinating graduate course at Cornell University. The professor had developed a method for what he called "unpacking the structure of knowledge." Students in this class represented a wide cross-section of the Cornell graduate student population.

We each were assigned the task of presenting something important from our own discipline to the rest of the class. Then all of us together would try to unpack the essential elements and see the common threads across disciplines.

Enrolled in the class were students of writing, physics, mathematics, economics and biology, among others. I was the resident representative of the field of psychology.

I did a presentation on sleep and dreams. As part of my presentation, I asked my fellow students to briefly share a dream or two. I remember being startled by some of the dream reports that I collected. What I hadn't expected, and what I now understand is common, is that the way we dream is strongly influenced by our waking way of thinking.

Most people's dreams are highly visual and have very little language in them. But a student who was submerged in her creative writing had dreams that contained a lot of written language.

Even more surprising, the mathematical genius among us reported dreaming in the language of mathematics. He said that he sometimes dreamed of formulas being written on a blackboard by an invisible hand. The numbers would appear much more rapidly than a hand would be able to accomplish. At other times, he said, mathematical concepts and formulas would be expressed as elements displayed in three-dimensional space.

The rest of us in the class were blown away by his descriptions of the quality of his dream life because it was so alien from anything we had experienced. Even beyond the content were the emotional experiences that he reported were part of his mathematical dreams. He was a little embarrassed to tell us that sometimes he became emotionally and even sexually aroused by the thrill of experiencing mathematical operations taking place effortlessly and naturally while he slept.

He said that, during the dreams, he would sometimes be convinced that he had discovered some great mathematical breakthrough. Sadly, however, the brilliant formulation usually either vanished completely upon awakening or turned out to be trivial and something he already knew.

After my presentation on dreams, he became interested in dream incubation. I explained some basic techniques and he decided to see if he could conjure up some dreams that might actually contain useful innovative mathematical breakthroughs. Before the end of the semester, he did report a couple of interesting insights that he thought might pan out.

The theoretical physicist in the class reported a dream that he had experienced about half a dozen times. He dreamed he was a molecule speeding through space at the speed of light. From this vantage point, he had achieved a level of insight regarding Einstein's theory of relativity that had eluded him before this dream. He told the class that his dream was like one that he had read Einstein himself had had during his youth. He said that Einstein asserted that this childhood dream had sent him on a course which culminated in his developing his world-transforming theory. However, I have never been able to find a source that independently confirms that Einstein actually had such a dream.

Speaking of Einstein's dream life, a collection of short stories published in 1993 by Alan Lightman entitled *Einstein's Dreams* presents a series of dreams that the young patent office clerk might have had during the time he was developing his revolutionary theories. The author is an MIT professor of physics and also of writing. The book is fascinating reading.

In addition to absorbing interests, a person's mental health and life situation have an important effect upon dream content and emotions.

Patients in a mental health facility have dreams that are consistent with their mental disorder. People in drug detoxification facilities or halfway houses trying to recover from drug abuse almost universally have dreams in which they have relapsed and are using their favorite drugs once again. They're usually very troubled by such dreams. But, at the same time, they enjoy the high which is often realistic and intense. Working with these dreams almost always results in the discovery, in the dream itself, of the wisdom and strength of the recovering person.

Seriously mentally ill patients have many confused and disorganized dreams. Such patients, especially those who have experienced vivid hallucinations, are understandably reluctant to even try to remember their dreams. One woman put it quite clearly when she said "I've spent many months trying to put the dreams that had haunted my waking life back in the box, and I'm not interested in opening myself up to those nightmares again."

Such reluctance should obviously be respected. But even seriously mentally ill patients can sometimes find new clarity and insight working with dreams. One young woman, who believed that her sister was out to kill her, dreamed that the sister was cleaning and bandaging an open wound in the dreamer's forehead. She concluded that her sister was only trying to help her "get her head back on straight."

Patients suffering depression or anxiety disorders often have dreams that reflect those moods. Depressed people sometimes have dreams set in dark underground rooms where there is little air and no way out. In one of my dream groups a woman made a straightforward statement that she intended to go back into just such a dream, and turn the lights on.

Of course, the nightmares of people suffering from post-traumatic stress disorder involve painful repeated intrusions of past traumas into present dreams. Sometimes, instructions for how to become more lucid in such dreams can help the dreamer begin to transform the dream from a nightmare into a memory, or maybe even a dream of acceptance and serenity. You may recall that a lucid dream is one in which the dreamer is aware, during the dream, that he is dreaming.

In an earlier chapter, I shared the dream of a prisoner at a maximum security facility and how he was able to transform his dream from a nightmare into a dream of transformation and hope. I will now describe a little bit more of what it was like to work with dreams in a class of hard-core, long-term prisoners.

I found prisoners to be very receptive to dream work. Perhaps finding oneself removed from regular life and trapped in an alternate universe leads to an increased willingness to look inside and try to understand the deepest parts of oneself. Maybe this willingness is also rooted in trying to understand the destructive and violent actions that landed the person in prison in the first place.

In addition to the sometimes startlingly insightful dream interpretation work, there was a second, equally dramatic, aspect of working with inmates.

The second aspect was the effect of dream work upon the relationships among the members of the class. After two or three sessions of sharing and exploring the meaning of symbols and the significance of emotional reactions, it became apparent to all of us that a special relationship was developing among members of the class.

While inmates of a prison know that they share a common fate and, in a sense, are brothers, there is a considerable and understandable maintenance of psychological distance between people in a place like prison. A maximum security facility is not a place where trust and intimacy are easily achieved.

In spite of the context, however, there were moments of important insights, and gestures of reaching out and a willingness to be vulnerable in the act of revealing dreams.

I don't want to overstate this case. A few hours of psychic touching, while important, must be viewed in the context of the ongoing 24-hour-a-day grim reality of prison life.

Toward the end of the semester, I asked students to share with me their views on the benefits of working with dreams as a tool for gaining personal insight. What follows are excerpts from a few of the responses. I share them here because they eloquently spell out the challenges and blessings of working with dreams.

"Dreams vary in intensity just as predicaments vary in importance, but dreams are often helpful indicators of just how intensely a predicament can be affecting a person. When our dreams relate directly to our predicaments, the intensity of the emotions that we experience often surprises us. Our dreams can drive home some pretty deep thoughts by caricaturing real situations, some of our weaknesses and some of our strengths. Our fears or hopes can be magnified through our dreams, and we can often be motivated by such dreams to change real predicaments."

"Many obstacles exist in prison life. Just to name a few: the deprivation of freedom, the dehumanization of one's being and the lack of control over one's self-direction. In dealing with these predicaments, one can either solve them rationally or expect them to continue. But with the help of dreams, one can see them start to diminish. There is no guarantee that dreams will be the ultimate cure to the problems that exist. However, dream work can be extremely helpful."

"Dreams, even those that image 'myths,' can be helpful. There is something to learn about ourselves in every dream, although the importance or significance of each dream that we experience will vary to some degree from dream to dream. Sometimes our dreams act as premonitions or portents or warnings; at other times, dreams help us to sort out realities or solve problems, or to simply make us feel good about ourselves, which can often be the greatest help to any of us. Understanding our dreams can eliminate fears, and many times fears are what keep us from succeeding."

"Dreams are obviously mental outlets and psychological tools provided for man by nature. They have a multitude of reasonable functions in the life of man, and they can manifest themselves in many ways. Perhaps, as we grow into greater awareness concerning the functions of the mind, we can understand better just how dreams serve us, and, in this particular case, how dreams can expose and help us to destroy detrimental personal myths. Only with a greater knowledge of dreams can we truly grow to understand the purpose and meaning of dreams in our lives, and perhaps even discover why we 'NEED' to dream."

The style of our dream life is also affected by specific experiences we have while we're awake. Watching movies is an experience that is a significant part of modern life, and there is an interesting relationship between night-time dreams and the cinema.

When dream group members are asked about what possibly led them to have a particular dream, they often say that they had been watching a movie earlier that evening and that the dream was probably the result. I usually try to steer such interpretations in the direction of looking at the personal associations rather than seeing the dream as simply a replay of the movie. But I think that this commonly perceived connection between the movie watching and dreaming is very real.

There are a number of reasons why movie content shows up in dreams. First of all, movies are watched in a passive manner. The filmmakers take the viewer on a sensory journey to a magic world. In contrast to other situations, a moviegoer is in an almost hypnotic state of heightened suggestibility. So it is no surprise that images from a recently seen movie would find their way into our dreamscape.

196

Another aspect of the connection between dreams and movies is that both involve unusual ways of experiencing the world. When we are wide awake, we have to get around by walking or driving a motor vehicle. In dreams, we are transported magically from one location to another, and even when we are moving around a room the movement is usually smooth and accomplished without noticeable footsteps. This is also the case in films, where the camera pans across the scene or moves us seamlessly from one location to another.

These are interesting common experiences shared by cinematic productions, a modern phenomenon, and the timeless process of dream creation. So it is not surprising that moviegoers find their night-time dreams sprinkled with images that they have recently viewed in the movie theater.

It is also not surprising that dreams are sometimes the inspiration for movies. For a while before their professional relationship disintegrated, Alfred Hitchcock consulted extensively with Salvador Dali about the dreamlike images in some of his films. Director Ingmar Bergman confessed that at least one scene in one of his films was lifted directly from his own dream life.

It seems that inspiration between dreams and films is a two-way street. Dreams inspire and enrich films, and because of their dreamlike quality, films lend their creative realities to our night-time dreams.

Chapter 21

Brain Chemistry and Spiritual Awakening

"The modern church is a great source of pain to me, because all it does is shamelessly speak of God." Carl Jung

Throughout this book, I have referred to the transformational power of self-hypnosis and dream work. I have described how these tools can help open a pathway between the conscious and the unconscious minds and how the results can change a person's life.

In this final chapter, I will talk about two very different ways of understanding these dramatic results. One way is spiritual. The other is biological.

I and My Brain Are One

Modern science has increasingly turned to the study of the brain as a way of understanding how we humans think, feel and act. This way of studying the brain, and trying to change our minds by changing the brain, has proven very successful. There are scores of psychiatric medications that can have profound results. They can greatly alter thoughts, moods and behaviors by tinkering with brain chemistry. And we all know how seductively and destructively certain drugs of abuse affect people's lives by changing their brains in negative ways.

Is there any evidence that the techniques we've been discussing can also affect brain function, chemistry or even structure?

The biological perspective assumes that every psychological and even spiritual experience has its roots in the biochemistry of the brain. Powerful hallucinogens like magic mushrooms, peyote and LSD directly manipulate what's going on in the brain. The results, however, are experienced by the user as dramatic changes in the way the world is perceived.

Similarly, many seriously mentally ill patients report vivid and disturbing psychological experiences that turnout to be the direct result of abnormalities in brain structure or function.

Surprisingly, we also have learned that people suffering from a wide range of disorders are really suffering from too much memory. Just as an Alzheimer's patient is rendered helpless by a lack of memory, these other sufferers are overwhelmed by memories they can't forget. This is obvious with post-traumatic stress disorder but is also true for things like depression, anxiety and obsessive-compulsive disorders. In all these cases, the brain seems to be etched with memories that cause sadness, pain and fear.

More than 20 years after returning from Vietnam, Randy still suffered from terrifying nightmares and powerful startle responses. Any time he was surprised or there was a sudden noise, his body would be kicked into a state of high alert. Randy enrolled in my course on hypnosis because he was both curious about the content and hopeful that he might learn some techniques that could help.

He began practicing a number of self-hypnotic procedures in order to give himself direct post-hypnotic suggestions. This didn't seem to do him much good. I had recently reviewed some studies that showed the effectiveness of individually constructed stories for giving oneself indirect posthypnotic suggestions. The results were shown to be especially effective in cases of PTSD.

So we decided to create our own scripts. We worked closely together to come up with scenarios that fit his traumatic experiences and his current emotional disturbances. After only a few weeks, the results were dramatic.

The results that Randy achieved are consistent with the considerable research pointing to actual brain circuitry changes that take place after consistently using indirect posthypnotic suggestions. The research is exciting and brings hope to many people.

In recent years, a number of popular psychology and self-help books have been published saying something like "change your thinking and change your brain," or "change your behavior and change your brain chemistry," or "think your way to mental health." All of these ideas have good research behind them. And I believe that the best science supports the use of self-hypnosis and guided imagery as among the most effective ways of changing long-standing brain chemistry-related difficulties.

Of course, there are other ways of influencing a brain that has gone awry. Taking psychiatric medications is one of the most direct methods. Somewhat less direct are things like getting the right amount of sleep, as well as proper diet and exercise. Even more indirect but important, are things like maintaining social connections with family and friends, and managing stress.

I don't want to leave this part of our discussion without pointing out that the view that the brain is the master of our destiny is based on a powerful model of what it means to be a human being. According to this model, we are animals, biological creatures pure and simple.

I and the Father Are One

There is a second worldview, however, that for many people is powerful and compelling. This view understands the essential nature of human beings to be more than a collection of biological processes. In this worldview, we are essentially spiritual beings. This does not imply any particular religious orientation or dogma. People with many different spiritual orientations hold this view. There is no doubt, however, that faith can heal, that faith can transform lives and that spiritual insight and development can bring people serenity and moral virtue in ways that are difficult to find in any other context.

The opening quote of this chapter assumes this point of view. In it, Carl Jung, complains about the lack in many churches of a first-person experience of the divine. Jung believes that mental and spiritual health depends upon a sense of a connection with the mysterious underlying power of the universe, whether we call that God or not.

Over the years, I have seen self-hypnosis and dream work stir experiences of a connection with the sacred. These experiences vary depending on one's background and religious sensibilities and beliefs. But the common thread is one of becoming more deeply conscious and in touch with the source of all being, however one might experience that. Many people call it God. But even that term leaves the question of which God or what kind of God are we experiencing. People who have had these kinds of experiences often don't care much about the theological details because the experience itself has been so powerful.

What follows is the case of a young man with a particular religious orientation who had a mystic experience through doing dream work.

Justin grew up in a good home. His parents were hard-working and kind. But he would later say there was a lack of joy there.

When Justin was 14, he attended an evangelical Christian church with a schoolmate. He described how during the first service he became restless and distressed during the altar call. He said that he felt so torn between a desire to go forward and an urge to stay put that he almost ran out of the church.

In an evangelical church, there is an altar call at the end of the service. It is the time when those present are asked to come forward and confess their sinfulness and need for the saving grace of Jesus. It is a simple declaration of faith and belief: Belief in the divinity of Jesus as the Son of God and in his redemptive sacrifice on the cross to save all humankind. And it is an act of personal faith and commitment to being born again in the spirit.

Many would argue with the theology behind the altar call and all that it implies. But this act of private and public confession and acceptance of Jesus as personal savior has been an exquisitely simple and profoundly effective moment in the lives of countless souls.

During the second service he attended, Justin answered the call and came forward. And for the next five years he had an on-again off-again relationship with both the church and with Jesus.

Justin attended a series of Bible study classes and spent several summers at Christian camps. But still he struggled. He said that he was troubled by doubts and that his beliefs sometimes felt shaky. But that was not the crux of the problem. He was most disturbed by his inability to really feel the presence of God. He felt a closeness with his Lord during the first few months after his conversion, but the experience faded and he was unable to get it back.

Justin enrolled in my sleep and dreams class because, although he rarely remembered his dreams, those he did remember were gripping and emotionally intense. He stopped by my office and we discussed the possibility of him using some techniques of dream incubation to see if they might help him out of his sense of being in spiritual limbo.

Justin was submerged in a very busy life. He was attending school full-time, had a 30-hour-a-week job, and was helping his mother care for his father, who was passing slowly into the darkness of Alzheimer's Disease. So he only had the energy and time to start with the minimum dream incubation procedure. He began by using the phrase, "I yearn for God's presence in my dreams." After about two weeks, Justin was getting frustrated. He not only did not have any dreams that spoke to his spiritual yearnings, but he wasn't remembering dreams at all.

I reminded him of the fact that sleep deprivation usually results in very little dream recall. As it happened, the college was about to go on spring break and Justin was determined to get more sleep and to move on to the more elaborate dream incubation techniques I described earlier.

A couple of weeks later, Justin phoned me to tell me that on the third night he had a life-changing dream experience. He also told me that, the very next day, his mother was critically injured in a car accident and that he had dropped out of school because as an only child he had become the primary caregiver for both of his parents.

Some five years later, he wrote me a letter from across the country where he had moved following the death of his parents. He said that the spiritual awakening from his incubated dream had gotten him through many dark months. What follows are excerpts from his letter to me, describing the dream and his understanding of it.

"I'm in a brightly lit room and there is a shrill and intense sound. I'm naked and shivering. I recognize this place as being familiar but I can't remember why. I begin to feel as though I'm going to die. I can't get my mind to think clearly about how to escape from the cold and the bright lights and the deafening sound. I become aware that I'm not just cold because the air is cold, but I'm cold because I'm lying on a cold surface. The surface is shiny stainless steel, and although I can't seem to think the words, I know that it is what it is. I desperately need help, but everybody seems to be attending to someone else. I begin to recognize the shrill sound as a baby wailing and gradually come to realize that I am the one crying. I can't comfort myself and nobody comes to my rescue. Now I'm feeling more strongly that I'm going to die, and my panic deepens.

"At this point, I experience my own second, observing consciousness as though I'm both on the stainless steel table and also watching from across the room. As I look on, I realize that I'm watching the scene right after my caesarean birth. I had always heard stories about how my mother almost died from the operation and had to be repeatedly revived. I now realized that I am re-experiencing that scene, when everyone was so busy saving my mother that I must have been left unattended for a while. But I also realize that this scene means more than just the reliving of a memory. It also perfectly depicts my sense of being lost and abandoned in a world without the experience of the presence of God.

"Then suddenly, someone is there and I feel the warmth of an embrace. At first I think that a nurse or someone has come and picked me up. But I realize that I am still lying on the cold table but somehow am no longer cold. Yet I feel the warm embrace of a loving caregiver. I'm baffled. Then I see him and feel him at the same time. At first, the image of Jesus is foggy and faint. But as I watch and feel the image, it is both across the room and, at the same time, holding me with a full-body, warm embrace.

"I begin to wake up into my bedroom, but the experience of the Lord's presence remains vivid and comforting. I am now wide awake and grab my dream journal, go into the kitchen and begin writing.

"I wept and wrote for over an hour. I don't know whether or not this dream captured a true memory or a fantasy memory. But, either way, I now know with certainty that Jesus has been with me all along and protecting me for my entire life. Long before I first heard His name, He was there. I have just been too blind and insensitive to feel His presence. Since this dream, I have never lost the deep conviction that He both holds me in his embrace and walks beside me every day."

Such an amazing dream needs no further explanation.

While perhaps not as detailed or powerful, I have listened to scores of accounts of what Carl Jung would call big dreams that have been life-altering. Regardless of your religious orientation it is possible you could have your own spiritually enlightening and comforting dream experience.

The Journey Continues

So we have, for now, come to the end of our journey together. I would be satisfied if you have found this journey to be informative, interesting and entertaining.

I would be even more satisfied if you choose to continue this journey alone or with others by using the tools described here to more fully appreciate and explore the wonders and creativity that remain locked inside your unconscious inner mind.

And beyond that, my hope is that you are successful in penetrating deeply enough into your unconscious mind to bring about some changes in your brain as we have described them.

Or perhaps you will break through into a spiritual awareness in keeping with your own beliefs and commitments. As I have said, I've have seen this happen many times over the years.

In addition, my hope is that, as you do this work, you will gaze deeply enough into your own mind to find the rest of humanity welcoming you into our shared reality, our shared destiny.

We live in an age when many men and women are becoming aware that we are all in this together, not only as human sisters and brothers, but also including all living beings and the earth itself. I believe that this work can make a contribution to this evolving awareness.

At a number of points in this book I have mentioned my website, www.hypnosisdreams.com. . I hope you will join me and other readers and hypnosis, sleep and dream enthusiasts in our discussions and explorations. Available on the website are many recordings I have prepared to help you in your hypnosis, sleep or dream related work as well as additional sources and links for further reading and knowledge.

Acknowledgments

I am grateful to the many people who have, over the years, shared their personal stories and dreams with me as students, dream group members and clients. I am also in debt to those who have done me the honor of placing their faith in me as a hypnotist. This book would not have been possible without their participation.

Many friends, family members and colleagues have encouraged me in the writing of this book. Others have read and given me feedback and criticism for its improvement. I would like to thank them all.

Most significantly, my wife Susan was an ongoing source of encouragement and often lifted me out of the writer's slumps that stymied me from time to time. As a former newspaper editor Susan's expertise was invaluable. But even more importantly, Susan insisted that I strive for a style that would make <u>Your Genius Within</u> readable and engaging. I believe that, working together, we achieved that goal.

I would also like to thank Meredith Maslich of *Possibilities Publishing* for so competently attending to all of the complex details involved in getting a book into print and available electronically. Meredith also set up and developed the website and blog hypnosisdreams.com. The outstanding quality of these finished products speaks for themselves. Meredith is a true professional in every way.

About the Author

Victor P. Garlock, Ph.D. has taught psychology and education courses at a community college, a liberal arts college, a private vocational institute, and a maximum security prison. Among many other college-level courses, he has taught classes on sleep, dreams, hypnosis and meditation.

He earned his doctorate from Cornell University where he was also a researcher in the department of psychology and the graduate school of education.

Dr. Garlock has conducted enrichment programs for elementary, middle and high school students on the topics of sleep and dreams. He has also led in-service workshops on hypnosis and stress management for hospitals, community mental health centers and private corporations.

As a psychotherapist Dr. Garlock has utilized hypnotherapy and dream interpretation in this work for over 30 years.
As a consulting hypnotist Dr. Garlock has worked with professionals in the fields of medicine, dentistry, sports and law enforcement among others.

30736473R00115

Made in the USA
Columbia, SC
29 October 2018